CONVERSATIONS
WITH
ACTORS

D1566108

Passion is the universal humanity. Without it, religion, history, romance, and art would be useless.

—Honoré de Balzac

CONVERSATIONS
WITH
ACTORS

on Film, Television, and Stage Performance

CAROLE ZUCKER

HEINEMANN
Portsmouth, NH

Heinemann
A division of Reed Elsevier Inc.
361 Hanover Street
Portsmouth, NH 03801–3912
www.heinemanndrama.com

Offices and agents throughout the world

Library of Congress Cataloging-in-Publication Data
Zucker, Carole.
    Conversations with actors on film, television, and stage performance / Carole Zucker.
        p. cm.
    ISBN 0-325-00372-6
    1. Acting. 2. Actors—United States—Interviews. 3. Actors—Great Britain—Interviews.
I. Title.

PN2061 .Z83 2002
792'.028—dc21   2001039295

Editor: Lisa A. Barnett
Production coordinator: Elizabeth Valway
Production service: Denise Botelho, Colophon
Cover design: Darci Mehall, Aureo Design
Typesetting: LeGwin Associates
Manufacturing: Steve Bernier

Printed in the United States of America on acid-free paper
06 05 04 03 02 01 VP 1 2 3 4 5

To Mario

You are the call and
I am the answer
You are the wish
and I the fulfillment
You are the night
and I the day
What else
It is perfect enough
you and I
what more?

—D. H. Lawrence

Contents

Introduction

The impulse guiding *Conversations with Actors on Film, Television, and Stage Performance* was to challenge, or at least throw into question, a commonplace view that British and American actors represent two divergent approaches to performance. This distinction is articulated by two of the actors interviewed for this book:

> What we're great at is this kind of organic, shoot-from-the-hip, react-off-the-other-person, casual arena of acting. What we're not so good at is the control—voice work, interpretation, clarity, being able to use the text. . . . It's what the English are so good at, and why we love their theater.
>
> **—Lindsay Crouse**

> It's a very complicated relationship between the British actor and the American actor. There's a kind of mutual envy and a mutual inferiority complex. American actors tend to think the Brits are the great stage actors, and the Brits tend to think the Americans are the ones who act truly from the guts.
>
> **—John Lithgow**

The underlying implication of these statements is that British actors are technically proficient, but—compared with Americans—lacking in raw emotional power. It is the purpose of this book to assert that these generalized and reductive notions do not begin to account for the vigor, authority, complexity, and emotional depth of performances by British actors, or for the technical aptitude and artistry of American performers.

In British actor training, where technical excellence and control are stressed, views concerning self-revelation and access to emotional truths do, in some cases, depart from the more visceral, direct American approach. In preparation for this book and to better comprehend actor training (in addition to being an acting teacher myself), I audited classes at a number of acting schools in the United States and the United Kingdom. Among the schools I visited were The Neighborhood Playhouse, The Actors Studio, HB Studios in New York and the London Academy of Music and Dramatic Art, the Royal Academy of Dramatic Art, the Central School, and the East 15 in London, as well as the Bristol Old Vic Theatre School. One need only glance at a typical prospectus for a British drama school to note the enormous differences between British and American actor training. Among the items listed in the core curriculum for the Bristol Old Vic are, for example, improvisation, verse, stage combat, accent and dialect, singing, theater history, mime, tap, ballet, camera presentation, theater in education, makeup, radio work, and, of course, multiple classes in rehearsal and performance. Syllabi for acting classes in the United States are extremely limited by comparison. But while learned technique is crucial, there is also that enigmatic, innate, unique gift that an actor of stature must possess—talent. Tom Conti says,

> The part of acting that makes it interesting is the complicated part you can't teach. That's what makes De Niro or Hackman, or people of that ilk, great actors, and eminently watchable. There's a bit that they know that most actors don't know. You can't teach that bit.

Acting is largely an art of self-portraiture, and actors are universally required to draw on their personal resources—emotional, mental, physical, and spiritual—to develop and enact an interpretation. The route taken to formulate and express that interpretation will vary from performer to performer. And as the interviews in this book emphasize, the end product, whether British or American, is the emergence of a living, breathing, truthful creation, forged from the melding of technique, imagination, and instinct.

The acting we are most familiar with on both sides of the Atlantic is vastly influenced by the teachings of Constantin Stanislavski (1863–1938). The famous Russian actor, director, and teacher rebelled against the artificial codes of stage performance valorized in the nineteenth century. Stanislavski taught that acting has to arise not from externalized, premeditated behavior, but from the inner world of the character, what he called the "logic of emotions" in a given text. The character is then brought to life through the technical skill, invention, and immediate responsiveness of the actor, who creates a full, vivid, emotionally, and physically true portrayal of a character.

Although Stanislavski developed a style of acting that is often called "realistic" or "naturalistic," the Russian teacher never espoused the strictly accurate replication of human behavior; he emphasized the poetic and imaginative dimensions of that behavior. The truth that Stanislavski advocated is the probing, honest, deeply felt interpretation of a character's feelings and actions. It is that search for truthfulness and being present fully in the moment that guides and inspires the actors who speak in this book. As Helen Mirren says, "Don't think. Be."

The interviews probe the creativity that informs an interpretation and the intimate process whereby performers draw on their personal resources to develop and enact an interpretation. The actor deals with inanimate words on the pages of a script or play, and the process by which language becomes action is complex. First, actors need to be able to play their instrument—themselves—with skill and precision, an ability that requires training, practice, and discipline. Next, actors must comprehend the meaning of the words they speak, in all their amplitude. The text will most likely communicate the character's background, attitudes, beliefs, and relationships to others. Critical as well, are the ideas and feelings that circulate below the surface of the text—the subtext—the implied or possible meanings of the written words, that suggest the character's emotional journey. To find the colors with which to create a vital portrait, actors engage in an exploration of the self—their own individuality as artists and human beings. This knowledge and awareness will be filtered through technique, imagination, and artistry in order to inhabit and illuminate the world of the fictional character. This is the process many actors in the book refer to as "personalization," the search for personal experience and feelings that correspond to the emotional spirit of a character. It is the combustion of the actor and the character that will produce a performance. The actor fuses the flood of feelings and sensations that belong to the character with the truth of their own feelings. The actor, unlike the musician, or the painter, or the sculptor, is the instrument; there is no mediation between the actor and the character. Those feelings and sensations come through the actor, and he or she must be open, aware, skilled, and inspired enough to allow this process to take place. It is a common perception that actors are somehow estranged or distanced from the truth. As Lindsay Crouse says, "People think I practice telling lies all day, until I'm so good at it that you can't tell the difference. But that's exactly what acting is not . . . [it's] the struggle to bring out the truth of your being, the fullest dimension of yourself." Acting is not pretending, but *being*, having the craft and the courage to let the truth of the moment filter through you.

Above all, acting is a shared experience; actors must communicate to an audience. They are engaged in a relay of human feelings—their own, their characters, and those of the audience—feelings that are, at base, universal in their meaning. In that space of universal, shared experience lies the power and beauty of acting. Actors have the privilege of revealing profound truths to us about the human condition and, ultimately, about ourselves.

In speaking with the actors represented in this book, I found no common prescription for acting, but rather an eclectic mix of techniques and strategies. What unites all of the actors I interviewed is some combination of playfulness with seriousness of purpose, intelligence, passion, and imagination at the service of any given project. Universally, I found the subjects in this book to have a unique openness to experience, a quality that is at the core of all creativity.

When I conducted these interviews—gathered over a period of several years—I established certain parameters. I usually entered into the conversation with a list of performances I thought were key, or fruitful for discussion. I was not concerned with the *latest* or most widely honored performance, but with what underlying lessons an actor might impart about his or her process, beliefs that would be of lasting and universal value, rather than representative of a momentary peak of achievement. I often discarded my "script," as I felt it was important to respond to the integrity and spirit of the individual's personality, rather than to commandeer the interview process. The responses on the part of the actors were, of course, highly individualized, and they naturally invested the greatest energy in subjects of personal significance to them. Some actors wanted to discuss their process; some wanted to talk extensively about their training. Still others warmed to larger ideas, for example, the dimension of storytelling that informs acting, the place of the actor in society, or the meaning of stardom. In the case of the British actors, I was provoked by Glenda Jackson's statement, "I don't think the English are particularly concerned with making heroes and heroines out of actors and actresses." This attitude—quite at odds with the American hunger to mythologize and to demonize actors—seemed characteristic of a British perspective which finds something slightly distasteful about fame, and standing out from the crowd. This idea made its way into my discussions with British actors—the possibility that a national outlook would impact on performers. Equally, the multicultural aspect of British society came into play in interviews with Indian actor Roshan Seth and New Zealand–born Kerry Fox. In each of these cases, their heritage is clearly of great importance, and became integrated, of necessity, into the interview process.

Although acting may grow out of an abstract concept like inner truth, the interviews in this book are based on the premise that acting can be investigated in a pragmatic and useful way. The actors were asked about their training, preparation for a role, and experiences of rehearsing and performing in various media. One of the purposes of the book is to explore the real or perceived differences between American "method" acting and British classical acting. This became a major thread, particularly in the interviews with British actors. *The* twentieth-century art form—film—is deeply embedded in the American psyche; image culture is unquestionably dominant in the United States. The camera loves to watch behavior and thought. The British film industry is much more artisanal and smaller in scale, and not so pervasive an influence on their cultural landscape. On the other hand, the British have an incredibly rich legacy of history, language, and theater, to which we in America can never aspire. And theater, by its nature, is bound up with language (unless we are talking about spectacle theater like *Les Misérables* or *Phantom of the Opera*). The British emphasis on text and the significance Americans give to what might be called "behaviorism" inform the nature of performance in each culture. Helen Mirren makes this controversial statement:

> I think the thing that is remarkable about American actors, although it's both remarkable and it's their great downfall, is that they jump very easily into emotion, which is great. Their facility to reach into an emotional well, and just jump headfirst in, and be unashamed and unafraid of doing that, is remarkable and admirable. However, the down side of that is that it is facile. It's facile emotion, it's not real, it's false. It's a sort of a reproduction of an emotion.

That said, a great many of the American actors represented in this book (John Lithgow, Christine Lahti, Lindsay Crouse, Richard Dreyfuss) have achieved great success on stage, while many of the British actors (James Fox, Kerry Fox, Roshan Seth) work primarily in films. As Richard Dreyfuss says, ". . . you just remember what court you're on." Tom Conti sums up the mastery of performance—whether in film, in television, or on stage—when he says, "The trouble with actors is that they act. The skill is *not* to show the acting." The final goal of performance is to be fully present in the moment, whether one is a "method" or classically trained actor. It is the core and essence of each of these interviews, as it is at the heart of all great performance.

Finally, I would like to extend my gratitude to all of the actors who generously donated their time to this project. Their warmth, openness, and gracious hospitality made writing this book an extraordinary privilege.

Carole Zucker
Montreal, Canada

Abbreviations for Actor Awards

An *N* after the name of an award indicates that the actor was nominated but did not win.

AA - Academy Award, awarded by the Academy of Motion Picture Arts and Sciences

BAFTA - British Film Academy Award, awarded by the British Academy of Film and Television Arts

Cannes - Cannes Film Festival Award

GENIE - Awarded by the Academy of Canadian Cinema and Television

GG - Golden Globe Award, awarded by the Association of Foreign Journalists

Obie - Off-Broadway Theater Award

Olivier - The Laurence Olivier Award, awarded by the Society of London Theatre

SAG - Screen Actors Guild Award

Tony - Antoinette Perry Award, awarded by the American Theater Wing

Emmy - Awarded by the National Academy of Television Arts and Sciences

Lindsay Crouse

You're very translucent when you're on film. You are a figure of light; your soul comes through. You can tell, easily, when someone you see is really doing it or not.

CAROLE ZUCKER: *How did you train to be an actor?*

LINDSAY CROUSE: When I first decided to become an actor I was doing something else. I was very busy trying to become a dancer. I was dancing and rehearsing dances—dancers rehearse forever, they perform very little. Dancers learn the dance and go out and perform it. Nobody coaches you on the difference between rehearsing and performing. So, when I got on stage, I had all these actors' questions. What happens if I don't feel like it? What is my relationship to the people on stage? What is my relationship to the audience? What happens if I forget something?

I began to do showcases in New York, off, off, off Broadway, in the Bowery, in horrible little theaters, where there was usually some bum getting warm, or my mother in the audience, and the director. They were wildly melodramatic plays, and they required that I really throw myself in. With these questions—whether or not they were answered—it became clear what I needed to know. At that point, I decided to go to acting class.

I went first to the Stella Adler Conservatory. I began to get a sense of what it was simply to put myself in imaginary circumstances and live truthfully in them. And I enjoyed the experience. I thought, well, wait a minute, I want to explore more about this acting stuff, so I went and studied with Sonia Moore at The Stanislavski Studio. This was a very different, much more formal approach, and one I didn't always understand. It didn't seem to be the school for me. Whereupon I went to the HB Studio. I liked it so much that I thought, now I really want to go to the top here. So I auditioned for Uta's [Hagen's] class and got in. That was really the beginning of my formal training. The others were explorations.

Uta obviously had defined acting for herself, and was in the process of writing her book, *Respect for Acting*. In her classes you came on time, and you were quiet, and you had your work prepared. You did it in a very professional manner, and you were critiqued by her. The moment I stepped into her class, I felt that was the beginning of my being an actor.

CZ: How long did you study with Uta Hagen?

LC: I was in and out of Uta's class for seven years. I would work and come back, and sometimes take class while I was working. At a certain point, because of personal conflicts, I came into such crisis that I became progressively paralyzed. You can see it on screen in things I was performing that year, until finally I felt that I was looking at a dead person. I was in such crisis, I thought, "Something is really wrong at the bottom here." I have got to find out what acting is, from the source.

I decided I would go and study with Sandy Meisner at The Neighborhood Playhouse. This was in the midst of having had an Academy Award nomination [*Places in the Heart*, 1984] and being a very successful actress. So I went to Sandy, and I said, "I realize that I am not a beginner, but I would like to be admitted to your beginners' class. I promise I won't put on airs. I'm coming like an acolyte. I want to stand at this altar and find out what this is." And I explained my crisis to him, and he said, "Never learn acting in performance." I said, "Well, I'm guilty. I'm submitting, I need correction."

CZ: What were the basic differences between Uta Hagen and Sandy Meisner's teachings?

LC: I would say that Uta had personalized her technique of acting. She did studies, for instance, on how to portray cold and heat, how to wake up on stage, how to wait, how to talk on the telephone. Very basic, technical exercises. There was an exercise in which you would bring in what the character had in his pockets or in her purse. It was always a fun exercise to do. Uta would say, "Keep a book on your character, as you're preparing. What kind of music does the character like best? Where does the character go to school? What would he wear to school? What was his favorite birthday gift?" She would say, "This may not appear on stage, but you will carry it in with you as a cloak of authenticity when you walk in the room. You will have fleshed out the character; you will have painted a three-dimensional picture that will ground you."

For emotional preparation, Uta had her own theory about an actor having an objective and an obstacle in a scene. And you define the obstacle. That was her thing. Of course there's an obstacle; that's what makes the scene dramatic. The obstacle is provided by a writer, and by the other person in front of you, who you want to get something from, who wants to get something different from you. One of the things that I found happened to me in her training—being a very conscientious person with a very strong will—was that I could perform an obstacle in spite of just about anything in front of me. I was so hellbent to get what I wanted that I would often railroad things that were really happening in a scene. There were a lot of things happening on stage which the audience must have been aware of and said, "Wait a minute, she didn't even see that. What's going on?" I was missing the boat in a lot of ways. I was performing a play, and I had decided what it meant, where the big moments came. I was choreographing my performance, which is the way a lot of actors work. I would never claim that Uta taught me that, but I would say that the technique somehow allowed that.

That was the biggest difference between Uta and Sandy. Uta would ask questions like, "How do you feel about this person, what do you think this means here?" The technique was to help you arrive truthfully at what you had decided the scene was going to mean. With Sandy, you were in unknown territory. Because original experience only happens in the desert. You don't know what you're going to meet. If you place your attention on the other person, you will always know where you're at; you'll always know what you have to negotiate with. That was really the beginning of my saying, "Well, I just won't do this play like a steam roller. I show up in the first scene, and I don't know what's going to happen. I don't know when or where the big crisis comes. I'm on a ride here." That's what his training was rigorously based on, that working off another person.

CZ: Can you give me an example of an exercise you did in Meisner's class?

LC: I remember one exercise where you have to repeat a phrase; it's a magnificent exercise. It puts you in something like an isolation tank; because there's so little stimuli, you notice any little thing that happens. I was doing this exercise with another actor; I thought I was doing rather well. And the actor sitting in a chair next to me leaned back in the chair so that the front legs were off the ground. He put his hands behind his head, like this (gesture of boredom), and I just kept going, doing the exercises. Sandy stood up and said, "I am absolutely appalled. A gigantic change just happened in the person sitting next to you and you didn't acknowledge it." I said, "What do you mean acknowledge it? He's just sitting here." My experience was telling me, "Look, the person is sitting there. If he got up to go to the other side of the room, and was throwing things, that's a change." But I was so little attuned, and Sandy really fine-tunes his students. He gives you such an eye and ear for very specific vocal and body language, so that you play a scene with a lot of variety. Just being tuned into that other person and knowing that your next feat comes out of what they do, and not out of what you decided the scene means.

CZ: At this point in your life, what are your feelings about all your training?

LC: I've come to discover that there's value in all of it. There is certainly value in working off the other person. There's value in having the courage not to decide what a moment means.

Very often acting is Zen; you have to completely avoid the thing you are trying to do. Just as if someone asks you if you know a joke, suddenly you don't know one. It's exactly the same mechanism in the mind. If someone says, "Well, the script says you have to cry here." If you head right for crying and laughing, it's the last thing that's ever going to come out of you. You have to perform a kind of mental acrobatics on yourself. That is what all this teaching is meant to unlock. People have different ways of doing it. Do whatever is working at the moment. I used to be very correct in everything. A director once said to me as I was stuck high on an emotional pole, "Nobody is going to know how you got this scene." And that's true. If I have to run around the block, if I have to ask everybody to leave the set, whatever it is I have to do, that's the order of the day. Technique ultimately has to serve the artist.

CZ: I suppose that's something you arrive at after years of experience.

LC: One of the first things Sandy told me was, "It takes twenty-five years to make an actor. I'm not surprised you're confused, you've only been at it for fifteen." He is so right. This culture needs to know that acting requires real maturity, because character in life is no different from the character on the stage. People have to develop their character, and that takes time. Actors stand for things, and they have to stand for things in their lives before they can be really good actors. All these acting techniques are meant to develop the inner life of a person so he can bring something to the situation.

CZ: Where does discipline and control come into all of this?

LC: I believe that it's the biggest thing missing in American acting. What we're great at is this kind of organic, shoot-from-the-hip, react-off-the-other-person, casual arena of acting. What we're not so good at is the control: voice work, interpretation, clarity, being able to use the text. Lee Strasberg said, "The text is our enemy." Well, yes, but I'll be god-damned if I'm going to go out there with people paying to see me and not have worked like crazy on that text, to be able to speak it; to know that my voice has the range to handle it; to know that I have enough breath control for it. And that stuff is disdained in this country. It's what the English are so good at, and why we love their theater.

CZ: When you first began making films, did you have any trouble adjusting to the camera?

LC: The biggest thing about film acting is that the physical restriction is just unbelievable. When I'm talking to you, in order to get a good angle, I can't really look at you; it's a tense thing. You need to see my face at some point, so I have to figure out where in the speech I can turn. Let's say I'm in a shot where my hand comes up, and I cleared my hair out of my ear in an earlier shot—which is the one we are keeping—we want to make sure I do it again, exactly then. If I hold a paper when I have to read something very important to you, the audience can't see it if it's down here, so I have to hold it at a totally unnatural height, like in advertisements for a product, but not appear unnatural doing it.

Film acting is like being in a tech rehearsal for a theater actor. It's those awful couple of days when they have given you the actual props, the actual coat, your hat. Something is too big, too small, something is not quite right. I remember this affected me a lot in Sidney Lumet's films, because Sidney has people eating a lot, and we wouldn't eat the stuff until we actually got to the shot. I suddenly found my mouth full of something either too wet or dry, too difficult to chew, or I was afraid something was in my teeth. It was hilarious because Sidney only does one or two takes of a scene. We had to deal with that stuff fast, and get it out of the way so that you could do your scene. There is a lot more improvisatory skill required to be a good film actor, because you're constantly in that situation where you never have it all together until the moment they say they're ready to shoot.

CZ: You've worked with Sidney Lumet on three occasions: Prince of the City *(1981),* The Verdict *(1982), and* Daniel *(1983). How does he rehearse with actors?*

LC: I'll tell you exactly how he works. It's brilliant, and every film director should sit up and take note. He brings his films in on time and under budget, and everybody goes home at five o'clock, has a good dinner and a good night's sleep for the next day's work. I took such a cold bath after those three pictures when I went to work for somebody else. I was on the set nineteen hours, no sleep, no meals, and overtime. Ugh!

Sidney most of all lets his actors know from the beginning that the whole thing depends on them. He is relying on you, and he enlists you as a colleague. Which is an incredible atmosphere to work in, because actors are always second-class citizens. He never refers to us as "talent." We are colleagues.

Sidney rehearses; he puts three weeks aside, and the first week he lets everybody rip. He encourages it. You can overact, you can talk loud, you can ask questions, you can wallow, you can whatever. Then, in the second week, he lets you know how the film is going to be orchestrated and what the tone of the piece is going to be. He'll say, "Now everybody got their rocks off and you're all loosened up, and you kind of know what you're doing. Now we need to figure out where the performance is going to lie."

One thing we did on *Prince of the City* that was so extraordinary is he sat everybody around this huge Italian banquet hall. He had the sets masking-taped down to the floor, and he had everybody get up and do their scene. He went from one person to another with the cameraman, as if he was filming the scene, and all the actors involved got to see all the other scenes they weren't in. And they got to see the scenes that went before and after their own. So you knew why Sidney was saying, "You're going to really have to hold back in your scene. It's got to be very intense, very quiet. Because before you there's this big chase, this shoot out, it's loud." So he let you see what the whole tapestry was going to look like, and you knew exactly where your piece fit. He wasn't going to waste time on the set, with you saying, "But I feel like it this way, I want to do it loud." He had you positioned precisely in the orchestration of that scene and you understood why. You want to give him what the big picture needs.

CZ: What if you disagree with him?

LC: You can talk to Sidney if you disagree with him. Sidney knows how to answer actors' questions. He knows how to keep actors fresh. What he does in rehearsal is he watches; he's a great watcher and a great listener. He observes your hottest performance in rehearsal; then he figures out how to get you there when you're on the set.

He does a brilliant thing. He often gives you a very small physical thing to do when you arrive on the set the day of your shooting. He'll say, "Oh, there's one thing I haven't mentioned which is, you've been up all night. Maybe dozed off for an hour." Let me be blowing my nose, or let me have a pimple on my ass and I can't sit down. Actors love that shit. He gives you something that's going to be fun to do, and is a little bit of a challenge. You are so busy thinking, "Oh, this is really fun now," it kind of relaxes your mind, so you aren't so intensely focused on "Will I fulfill this scene?"

CZ: Your role in The Verdict *as Caitlin was relatively small, but very crucial.*

LC: Yes, a powerful role. Sidney knew it was a role that required some control. I worked a long time with a voice coach to do that performance; I was doing an Irish accent. My text was "yes" and "no," until the very last moment of the scene. And my job in that picture was to be open enough to allow all that was going on in me, with the accumulation of those questions, to come out in those brief responses.

Now imagine you have the pivotal moment in the film, and you've got to go from A to Z in that scene. You know you have got to get to such a pitch at the end of the scene; it's like your whole life is breaking open.

That's a hell of a thing to walk in at five o'clock in the morning and know you have to do, and not clutch. That scene is one of the best pieces of acting I ever did. I discovered something which I still try to do with everything in me, with every part I do. Because I believe that great acting happens when what is going on in the scene dovetails exactly with something that you have to do in your life. It is your life in that moment. And that girl was making a confession. I worked to figure out what confession would be absolutely impossible for me to make, that I couldn't make in front of anybody. And I confessed that in that scene. And the event for me was cathartic. I made the confession, and I've never had to deal with it again. Now, you may see the scene and have your own interpretation of what I confessed. But what came out in that scene, universally, was a woman really confessing. That is a great performance no matter what meaning it has.

There's something interesting that happened in the performance of that part, I was very frightened that morning. I'd done one picture for Sidney, and this was my second opportunity with him. I would have died rather than not do a good job. The part was extremely intense. And I wanted to get everything out and not go home with it.

Sidney always calls you by your character's name when you arrive on set, which is very sweet, and he came up to me as I started the first take, and said very softly in my ear, "Caitlin, just talk, just open your mouth and talk." Which is, of course, the nature of a confession. The hardest thing is to open your mouth and talk. So I kept that with me. I didn't have to be a great actor. I just had to open my mouth and talk. The effort to do that was so moving.

Another thing in film is, you have to realize what the shot is for. Your master shot is probably for the opening of the scene and the end of the scene. You should ask, "What are you going to keep out of this shot?" They may let you run the scene in order to get to the end, so the end makes sense. You are going to have the over-the-shoulder shot, the medium shot, the close-up shot, and whatever else they decide to do. And that's going to take all day, maybe two days. And you are going to have to sustain. So you have to know where the emphasis is in the shot. Sidney had designed four different shots for this scene. He said, "O.K., we're going to do four moves in, closer, closer, closer, closer." So I knew that I had to do the scene four times. And each time he gave me a segment of the scene to do, and then the whole scene. And on the third move-in, we were really cooking, we went over the top. Everyone in the court room stood up. It was a great moment. And, he said, "O.K., new deal, let's move in," and I turned to him and said, "Sidney, I'm willing to do anything for you, but I just gave everything that I have, I don't know how I'm going to do it." And he came over to me and said, "That's O.K., we'll go on to the next scene." I thought that was very telling of Sidney's knowledge of acting—he realized he could get the closer angle, which was his plan for the scene—but why the hell do it if the actor had given one hundred and fifty percent? You really weren't going to get the same performance, even though you are going to get your angle. Not a lot of directors would have given up their plan and just gone with what happened.

CZ: Let's move on to Daniel. *It's based on the Rosenberg case, fictionalized in Doctorow's novel,* The Book of Daniel. *How much research did you do into the Rosenbergs and the period? Do you think it's necessary to do a lot of research for a role?*

LC: That's a good question. I think actors are very different on that score. I feel that to play any part, most of what is required is inside me. I also feel that if you are doing something very specific like that—it was a fictional thing, but it was based on historical characters and everybody knew it—I had to know what was up at that time. I read a great deal about it. I was amazed to see what they were doing, the way their whole lives were hung around the ideal of Communism.

I felt a great deal for Ethel Rosenberg and her situation, with the children in the midst of it. I think that she made an incredible thing out of her own situation. She was totally helpless, but she maintained her position to the last, for the sake of her children. So their memories, and the things they would read and hear about her, would consistently maintain her innocence and her dignity. She's one of my great, great heroes. I absolutely dedicated my performance to her, because I felt she had no spokesperson. It took three zaps to kill her, not for no reason. She was defying them. I said to Sidney before I began, "What do you think, was she guilty or innocent?" He said, "It doesn't matter, you're going to play her the same way. You have to step into her shoes, whether she was or not."

But I did do quite a bit of research on that film. I worked about forty hours with my voice coach to try to figure out how she talked. I felt it was really important to the credibility of the role, that she be placed in a context of an Orthodox family and Russian-Jewishness. Being cast in that role, I felt a great responsibility to be authentic. And not being Jewish, not being of a Russian background, not coming from that period, I tried very hard to enter it as much as possible so that nothing would interfere with people hearing her story.

CZ: The way the script is structured and the film is shot gives absolute sympathy to these people. I found the film very hard to watch, excruciating.

LC: It's brutal. I found it hard to play for the same reason. And I discovered in doing it, that when you play someone who you know is going to die, you're always overcome. You're always overcome by the aura of the script. And you always try to deny it. You play Othello and say, "Well, I can't play Othello because I feel so jealous, jealous of the other actors, jealous of the director." It sounds funny, but it is a phenomenon that happens over and over again. I thought I couldn't play the part in *Daniel* because everything seemed futile. I felt like I couldn't act. I drove Sidney quite crazy, because I kept saying, "I've got to rehearse this again." He'd say, "There's absolutely nothing wrong with this; you are doing beautifully." I'd say, "No, I'm not doing enough; I'm not there yet." And it's what I experienced during the entire piece, this accumulation of "I'm not doing enough," which was coming right out of the script. She was totally helpless, and she was a target, there's no doubt about it.

CZ: Can you talk about how you analyze a script and develop a character, relating it to the role of Rochelle Isaacson in Daniel?

LC: What I do is, first, look at the overall script and say, "This is a story about. . . ." I make one sentence of what the story is about. Then I take the character and I say, "What this character wants in the story is. . . ." And I make one sentence, "Rochelle wants. . . ." Then I lift the story of Rochelle out of the script. I take Rochelle's scenes and I type them out and staple them together: Rochelle's story. As if I were going to tell you in one sentence, "This is a story about a woman who. . ," and I describe the story. The first job I feel I have as an actor is to say, "You could read the story in a library. What am I going to give you that you couldn't get in a library reading this script?" My responsibility is the second thing, which is: What is it that I am really doing? Not what is Rochelle doing, but what am I doing? So, let's say this scene is—just an abstract scene I've made up—a character coming to get money from his father. But what I am really doing, the essence of that scene is, I'm coming to get restitution for a wrong done. O.K.? It's a little different from coming to get the money. What you get in the library is: "This is a scene about a character coming to get some money." But what you can't get in the library is the coming to get restitution. The third step is, what does that mean to me? Why do I have to get restitution, so that it is so important to me, I don't care if a million people see me do it. That's where the real work of acting lies. That's what I have to rehearse, getting restitution. So, I do those steps and what I feel happens is, the audience *sees* me getting the money, but they *feel* me getting restitution.

In life we never do what we say we're doing; that's why drama works so well. Some people call it subtext; to me, that's where the art of acting lies. Something has to come out of my mouth, which may be the opposite of what I am really doing. I have to be doing that second thing so strongly that you know it, and it's clear, even though I'm saying something entirely different. That's why Lee Strasberg says that your text is your enemy. Because in that sense, you are not there to act out the text. You are there to bring out, with all the force of your being, that action of the play. The through-action of the play, as Aristotle said; there's only one from beginning to end.

CZ: Can you think of an example from a film you've worked on where the words are different from the internal action?

LC: Sidney is wonderful at directing this way, because he knows the value of saying the opposite of what you are really doing. I saw him do the most brilliant piece of direction in a scene in *The Verdict*, in which James Mason has a Black actor on the stand, a doctor who has come to give expert testimony for the other side. James in this scene is supposed to really nail him, put him down. So he did the scene, he was unctuous, wonderfully evil; he was fine. I thought we would go on to the next scene. Sidney sat and thought a long time, and said, "James, dear"—he always called you "dear"—"I want to do it again. This time I want you to try something different. I want you to thank this man from the bottom of your heart, for coming here today, for taking the time to help everyone in this court-room get to the truth of this case." Well, you never saw evil so personified in your life, because that is exactly what evil is. And you knew why James Mason was the highest paid lawyer in Boston, and you knew why he had a following of twenty-five young kids, who wanted to work in his office. Because this man was the picture of courtesy; he was magnanimous; you couldn't find a hole in him. The guy on the stand started to squirm; he started to flub his lines. He was being nailed to the ground with such pre-cision and such tact! What James is saying in the scene is quite different from what he is doing. He is being extremely obnoxious to this guy who is trying to give his testimony. The brilliance of his direction was that Sidney understood very well that it would be far more powerfully played if he played it like a perfect gentleman thanking someone for coming to help. It released James from the obligation to act out the text, and made it a far more powerful scene. Because an actor will always want to act out the text. It's the easy thing to do; it's the obvious thing to do.

CZ: I remember when I was a kid, going to the Smithsonian Institute and seeing the Jell-O box on display that was supposedly used to transmit material between the Rosenbergs and David Greenglas. That cut-in-half box has always stayed with me as a reminder of the Rosenbergs.

LC: That's exactly the kind of emotional memory Uta Hagen talks about, something small, but extremely significant. Something on the floor, or a piece of lint on a curtain, she says you remember by some very mundane object, and that memory will trigger the whole emotion. She says when you have to act a very traumatic moment, sometimes the big moment is not when it happens to you. It's not the moment of death; it's when you have to take the key to the car out of your dead husband's pocket. It's something that surrounds it, that is so mundane, yet expresses all the pathos of the situation.

CZ: Your sympathies were with your character in Daniel*; what happens if your sympathies are not with a character?*

LC: Then you don't take the part. And chances are you won't get the part. Because you play roles that have resonance for you, where you can literally say—with every experience of your life leading up to that moment—"If this were happening to me, I would. . . . " Otherwise you cannot play with authenticity; you can't play with any kind of commitment to the part.

When I did *Places in the Heart*, I had a long talk with Robert Benton because my marriage vows were based on the fact that if my husband was unfaithful, I would leave him. And that he had a right to leave if that ever happened on my end. Here I had to play this part where I had to take Ed Harris back after he's made love to Amy Madigan. I had to really talk that over with Benton, because I felt that I had to truly understand that. Especially because the moment in which I take Ed back had no words, no speech; I had no way to get there. I had to communicate that silently and fully. I didn't want to play a part in which I felt I was doing something that was against my own values.

And I took a leap in my own life. I grew up by doing that part, in the sense that I took in the fact that there are things that can happen in a marriage, where indeed you would say, "We're going to wipe the slate clean. We're going to step over that and go on." I really possessed that by the end of the movie. I felt I was a bigger person because of it; I understood human situations better.

I also nearly lost that part because Benton wanted me to be nude in a scene. I didn't feel that it was warranted, and I said, "No, I can't do this." He said, "Well, I have to think about it then," because it was a very personal script for him. And I waited twenty-four hours thinking, "Maybe I'm not going to be able to do this film." But I stood by my conviction. I felt I really wouldn't be able to enter into the spirit of it. He called back and said, "O.K., we'll do it your way."

CZ: That was very courageous of you.

LC: It was. It might not be right for every situation, but you have to define what you can really get behind. You are a symbol on film for all people. Hopefully, the great ethic of acting is that you are going to do what you said you are going to do, no matter what. In other words, that I was going to take my husband back, no matter how self-conscious I was; even if I didn't feel like it that day. I had promised that I would get up there and offer forgiveness in that scene, and I had better bloody well do that. That's all we offer to people witnessing the story. If that woman can get up there and do that, when she has all this pain inside her, I can do that. You set an example, you're a symbol, so you had better be able to get behind it. Otherwise, I think it shows. You're very translucent when you're on film. You are a figure of light; your soul comes through. You can tell, easily, when someone you see is really doing it or not.

CZ: In discussing the ethical dimension of acting, the famous example is Falconetti in Carl Dreyer's The Passion of Joan of Arc *(1928). Dreyer did torturous things to Falconetti so she could get into the suffering of the character. And she ended up, after that experience, spending most of her life institutionalized. That's the archetypal story of something disastrous that can happen when an actor embraces a role very completely.*

LC: Well listen, I feel very strongly, and I teach my students this: You're either an actor or you're not. Even a beginning actor with no training can put themselves in imaginary circumstances, with all the truth of their being.

Taking on a role is a very tricky thing. And one of the things that technique is based on is protecting the human mind. As Sandy very elegantly put it, it's "as if" you are Jesus Christ, not that you are Jesus Christ. And there is a world of difference. Technique makes that extremely clear, and it is to train your mind to think in those terms, so that you yourself remain intact. That's what personalizing a role means, bringing yourself to that situation, not crowding out your own identity with another one. People say to me, "I don't know how you do what you do, I couldn't lie to save my life." People think I practice telling lies all day, until I'm so good at it that you can't tell the difference. But that's exactly what acting is not. As any acting teacher knows, it's struggling to bring out the truth of your being, the fullest dimension of yourself.

It's amazing how people will avoid using themselves in art, because we instinctively know that everything we do is a self-portrait. Acting is the art of self-revelation. We want to avoid that knowledge like the plague, because of all the ambivalence we have about ourselves. We are not good enough, we are not good looking enough, we're not whatever enough, so that if what we are doing is a self-portrait, everybody is going to see us. Oh my God, what will happen, then? Acting is like any great art; all you do is undo. The technique is to allow us to remove all that tension, self-consciousness, and all those defenses, all the reasons we say we can't step forward and shine. But what a great example when we do.

Acting is an art like any other, and art requires practice and control. Artistry requires craftsmanship. But the instrument is not some object removed from us; the instrument is us; and that's where the confusion lies. Because when you train an actor, you're training an actor's mind; you're creating thought patterns; you're creating habits of work, of thinking, of behavior. You want to deal correctly with that human being so that you focus solely on training an actor. Going to extremes is bull; that's someone who is not an actor. You don't have to cut your leg off at the hip to play a paraplegic.

CZ: House of Games (1987) is very different than the more naturalistic films you've been in. How did you go about developing the character of Margaret? What was the character's "through-line"?

LC: The character of Margaret wanted to serve; that's what I played in that film. She said, "I just want to do good." Her tragic flaw was that she wanted to serve to the point that she couldn't bear not being of service. The kid who comes into her office and says, "I'm going to die. What can you do about it? What do you know?" She can't bear the accusation. She has to help him. If she can't help him, her life is a lie; she doesn't know anything, and she's not of service. So, she has to help him, and that's what drives her to the "house of games."

CZ: Why does she have this obsession with being of service?

LC: Well, that's where the work comes in for the actor, what does that mean to me? That was something I didn't have to think about much, because I am that girl. That's the devotion of my life, and it causes me the same kinds of problems. That part had tremendous resonance for me, because I understand what it means to just want to do good. I think it is a very human motivation for living. But she was not equipped to help that boy; she should have turned that case over to somebody who knew about the situation.

CZ: But don't you need to know where that desire comes from within the character?

LC: All you have to know to play that person is that you are compelled to serve. And the "compelled" part comes from, "What does it mean to me? How important is it that I serve?" If you need to up the stakes of a script, a scene, you just need to find a better reason. If you have to do something and it's a chore, you could do it or not do it. But if you have to do something, and it's the most important thing you have ever had to do, you have to find a very good reason. If I have to come back in this house that's burning to rescue my daughter, I don't give a damn how many people are looking at me. If I have to come back to the house in order to get an extra key, it doesn't really matter. So in a script like this, where the woman is compulsive, you have to find a driving reason for her to want to serve that badly, to that extreme. She risks her life to help this kid; she goes to the "house of games" with these thugs. That's all that technique would require. She's a disintegrated person who's trying to integrate her sexuality. But that doesn't help you play her. All you really have to know to play her—you don't have to have sat in a psychiatrist's office, you don't have to study psychiatrists—is what it's like to need to serve so badly. And the effect is someone who doesn't think enough of herself, a person who feels compelled, a person who feels her life's a lie, a person who is finally rejected completely.

CZ: Margaret is an extremely controlled, repressed character. Was that difficult to play?

LC: People say, "Was that a really fun part to play?" And I say, "No." It's not a fun part to play, because that woman is probably the most passionate woman I ever played. A woman who wants to dedicate her life to service is a passionate person. But she couldn't show anything. The action that is in the script is very powerful. It's as if every day you went out to dig a ditch, and someone kept holding the shovel, and kept holding your arms back. And you keep saying, "I'm going to dig this ditch, I'm going to dig this ditch . . . ," so by the end of the project . . . whoa! She was in a straitjacket through the whole thing.

David's [Mamet's] direction to me constantly was, "Calm down, calm down, just talk in a normal voice, don't shout, don't show them anything." The essence of that character, and why it appears so stylized, is that she couldn't, she couldn't, she couldn't. And it drove us all nearly nuts. When you're doing it, your instinct is to constantly let the variety out, let her be . . . something. But the essence of her was that she was restricted. So it was interesting, but I wouldn't want to play people like that too much.

CZ: What about the language of the film? It's very ritualized and repetitious, and you're speaking almost in a sing-song voice. You must deal with it differently than you would a naturalistic text.

LC: Well sure, if there's a formal approach to something, there are many ways to justify that, internally. If it's a poem, there are many ways to justify that language. Uta gave me a great clue to this; she said, "Poetry is the most specific language that you'll ever speak." In other words, when Shakespeare says, "Make me a willow cabin at your gate, and fall upon my soul in your house," she says, "What Shakespeare's saying is, it's not a log cabin, it's not a concrete block cabin. It's a willow cabin, and only a willow cabin could possibly express the unutterable dedication of that girl who wants to camp out at the door of her lover." "Make me a willow cabin." God! It's so unbelievably delicate and so poignant an image. A poetic text is more specific than anything. And, therefore, you need to deal with it specifically; you have to give yourself specific reasons.

That language was terribly appropriate and gave the film a very strange life. David pared down everything to the essentials. That's why the film is so powerful and has such unity. Nothing is extraneous, not even the expression of the actors. It's bizarre, too, but highly poetic. David used to say to me, when we first talked about acting, "Everyone thinks my plays are kitchen plays, but they're operas!" And that gave me a great clue to David's work. Joe Mantegna appears to be, "Oh, I'm just shootin' the shit with Margaret here." But really, he's singing a song.

CZ: You teach acting. What is the most important lesson for future actors to know?

LC: The great example I can talk about as an actor is, most people spend their lives—and I'm including myself—taking an average. In other words, "Well, I'd really like to, but this is all I can do. If only I could save my mother, or, if I hadn't done that." We're filled with wishes. And the actor is meant to get out there and take themselves to the edge of the edge of the edge. To go as far as they can. I say to my students, "Don't take an average. If you're coming in to lay down the law, if you're coming in to get restitution, you get restitution! Let the playwright stop you. But until the last breath that you have, you do that with all the experience your life has given you up until now." Because everybody needs to be told that they can save their mother, that they can shoot for that dream. That's what all our stories are about. That's what all our myths are for. To take us to the next level, to say life can be better. You can change tomorrow what you thought you couldn't today. That's the leadership actors have, where they have taken people, as Joseph Campbell would say, "Into the forest of original experience." And they're going in themselves and then coming back to recount what it was like.

That's why when you see great acting, something happens which changes you, which is so overwhelming, so unbelievable, you don't have words. Everybody wants to be reduced to that level of zero by a great performance; that's what we're all studying these techniques to unleash. Truly, when you give a great performance, you don't feel it was yours; you feel that it came through you. That's the Zen of it. All you can do is prepare correctly.

Career Highlights

Film: *Between the Lines* 77. *Prince of the City* 81. *The Verdict* 82. *Daniel* 83. *Places in the Heart* (AAN) 84. *House of Games* 87. *Communion* 89. *Desperate Hours* 90. *The Indian in the Cupboard* 95. *The Juror* 96. *The Insider* 99. *Almost Salinas* 2001.

Theater: *Much Ado About Nothing* 72. *Hamlet* 79. *Reunion* (Obie) 79. *Twelfth Night* 80. *Childe Byron* 81. *Richard III* 82. *Serenading Louie* 84. *The Homecoming* (Theater World Award) 91. *The Tavern* 93. *With and Without* 95.

Television: *Paul's Case* 80. *Lemon Sky* 87. *Final Appeal* 93. *Out of Darkness* 94. *Parallel Lives* 94. *If These Walls Could Talk* 96. *Beyond the Prairie: The True Story of Laura Ingalls Wilder* 2000. *The Warden* 2001. Series: "Buffy the Vampire Slayer" 99–2000.

Richard Dreyfuss

*Every art form does something to the human soul in a differ-
ent way . . . but no art form can make you burst into tears,
or make you laugh by the immediate reflection of human behavior like acting can. And that's the nobility of acting. . . .*

CAROLE ZUCKER: *What first attracted you to acting?*

RICHARD DREYFUSS: I don't really know. I wanted to be an actor when I was
a tiny little child. I just knew I wanted to do it, and I did it. I started when
I was nine. I can't remember the why of this. It's the one question I've never
been able to answer. There's a lot about acting that I've come to know and
to love, but if you're asking my original impulse, I couldn't answer.

CZ: *You never had formal training, is that correct?*

RD: Yeah. I actually did apply and was accepted to both Yale and the London Academy of Music and Dramatic Arts, but the circumstances of the
draft in the late sixties were such that I didn't go. And I didn't take it seriously enough; it's one of the few regrets I have in my life. Because I think
that, especially with the ambitions I had to be a certain kind of actor, it
would have held me in good stead.

CZ: *Have you ever been coached by anyone?*

RD: Oh yes. When I was twelve years old, I found out that there was a
class in Beverly Hills in acting and improvisational techniques. The
teacher was a woman by the name of Rose Jane Landau; she was a very

formative influence in my life. It was a powerful thing to take, and I recommend it to all young actors. Because improvisational techniques not only teach you something about acting, they teach you about writing and directing. If you're really improvising smartly, you've got to know when to get on, when to get off, and what to say. It was very important in allowing me to become the actor that I am now.

CZ: Did you have an interest in films when you were growing up?

RD: One of the things that is different between the way I grew up, and the way people younger than me grew up—which I don't think has been acknowledged yet—is that when I grew up, I could see every single American movie ever made between 1929 and 1960 on American television all the time, seven days a week. Now you see one Warner Brothers gangster movie, for instance, on Nick at Nite, once. That was my training, other than Rose Jane, watching all those old films at three o'clock in the morning, over and over again. I deeply regret that we've become whoever it is we've become, that we can't make movies like this any more.

CZ: You've done a lot of stage work as well as film. What do you see as the major differences?

RD: In the theater, you get a sense of the whole; in film acting, you don't. When you're working on a movie, you're working in someone else's milieu, and you work out of sequence, and you work for thirty-second bites. I don't feel the same sense of completion in film, the sense of carrying a character from beginning to end. When you're working on the stage, you have a concentrated rehearsal of some four weeks, perhaps more, and then you perform every night from A to Z. So that's one major distinction between the two. The other is that the feedback you get in film is personal, it's intimate. You work with actors in a given scene, and everyone watching you is working; they're not watching you, they're working. Your feedback is from the other actors and from yourself. In theater, you're not only getting feedback from the actors, but you're getting feedback from an audience.

CZ: Do you think that the way the house feels each night influences what you're doing on stage?

RD: It doesn't necessarily, but it can. And sometimes you can affect them. In other words, you can start a performance at a certain energy level and bring the whole house up. You can start at another, lower energy level and the house stays the same, or sometimes their enthusiasm is so high that they goad you on. In film, in a sense, it's kind of self-generated.

CZ: What's the difference between theater and film in terms of movement and voice?

RD: Surely you have to carry the voice more strongly on stage, and you're in constant vision. But I don't really notice a difference. You work in a smaller way on film; the camera is right there, so that your eyes tell a lot of the story. In theater, if you let your eyes tell the story, then six people are going to know what the story is.

CZ: Do you feel it's a big adjustment for you to make, or is it very automatic?

RD: I was taking tennis lessons, years ago, and I said, "I also like to play racquetball, and I was told that the wrist movement was different; is this going to screw me up?" The coach said, "All you have to do is remember what court you're on." That's all, you just remember what court you're on.

CZ: Did you always have ambitions to become a film actor?

RD: The idea that I was actually going to make it as a star in America was a laughable idea to everyone but me. I thought it was a given. Everyone else said, "What, are you nuts?" But I knew it was going to happen.

CZ: When you watch your earliest performances, what do you see? And how do you view your evolution since then?

RD: It's hard for me to say. Some of my early work I think is pretty hideous. I did a lot of television, and I look at my television work now when it comes on, by accident, and it's amazing to me that I ever got another job. What also amazes me is how much I thought I was a great actor at that moment.

I don't really have a sense of my own "arc," as it were. There are individual performances that I like, and I like the later performances more than the earlier ones. I think I slowed down some and was willing to not hurry. I didn't need to be so energetic.

In the middle eighties, I became more willing to trust myself and to try other things, and slow down. I don't think I could have performed *Tin Men* (1987) in 1975 in the same way that I did later on, or *Stakeout* (1987), or *Let It Ride* (1989). I think in that way my work has improved. I'm not an actor who works well alone; I like to have a strong director, and I like to have rehearsal, and I like to have someone who will tell me, guide me, and say, "This is right, this is wrong." Most often, that doesn't happen.

CZ: Why not?

RD: Because directors no longer know anything about acting.

CZ: Why do you think that's happened?

RD: I think directing in movies is such a complicated, demanding position. He or she has to have a certain grasp of so many different things. They will say to an actor, "You know what you're doing? Good, because I've got to do all these other things."

I was speaking to Steven Spielberg one day—and other directors have mirrored this thought—I said to him, "What's your favorite part of directing?" And he immediately said, "My favorite part of directing is editing. Number one. My second is writing, my third is postproduction, my fourth is casting and preproduction, and my last, the one I have to endure, is shooting." I said, "Why?" and he said, "Every other part of it I can control. When I write, it's my fantasy; when I'm editing, it's my project," and so on, "but when I shoot, I've got to hand it over to other people, and it goes away, and becomes something else." I said, "Steven, never forget that the only time I'm around is when we're shooting."

There are directors, and fine directors, like Barry Levinson and George Lucas, who basically will say that their job with actors is done when they've cast the movie, which is unfortunate. Where a stage director creates a moment of timing, for instance, a film director will do that in editing. Oftentimes, I think my work would be improved if a director said something simple like, "You're talking too fast," or "You're moving too slow," or whatever. And for the most part, they don't.

CZ: Do you think it's true that directors are afraid of actors?

RD: Directors are inadequate about actors. There's a lesson to be learned; it's called "Actors 101." Directors should take a class not only in acting, but in actors, because the fears, anxieties, thoughts, wishes, or opinions that an actor has are pretty important to how the character is coming out. And the director should know how to do that. An actor, of course, should know also not to inflict his own bullshit on directors. That interaction can be improved; it's not there yet, not at all.

CZ: Who do you think directs actors well?

RD: I don't know. I have an idea in my mind of what the good director–actor relationship is. When Herb Ross and I did *The Goodbye Girl* (1977), that was the relationship I always thought actors and directors would have. He listened, he was funny, he was creative, he was intrusive. He said, "Get in here and do this and that." And we went back and forth, and it was very relaxed and happy, and he spoiled the shit out of me, he really did. I thought all directors were going to be like that.

CZ: What happens once you get a script in your hand?

RD: My "technique," as they sometimes say, is very mysterious to me. It's instinctual, it's not thought out. I'll read a script once, and I'll get a picture of the character in my mind, and then I'll try to be that picture. That's basically it. I normally don't do a lot of formal research. In other words, if I'm going to play a doctor, I don't feel it's necessary for me to go and spend two days with a doctor, although I might do it, just because it would be fun. It may be a failing of mine, but I didn't go and sell aluminum siding to play *Tin Men*. Most of it is in my imagination, and I try to achieve my imagination.

CZ: As the character Sam Sharpe in Once Around *(1991), you have a lot of complicated relationships with the family. Would you determine what your relationship would be with each character, or would that also be very instinctual?*

RD: I felt I knew him. The story of the movie is real simple: A girl falls in love with a guy who her family thinks is an egregious schmuck, and by the time they find out that he's more than an egregious schmuck, he drops dead. That's the story, and that's what he was. If a person is loudmouthed, over-bearing, whatever, it means he's blind. He doesn't see things, he sees what he wants to see. That's Sam; I knew that. It wasn't more intellectual than that.

CZ: What kind of rehearsals did you have for that film?

RD: We had some pretty good rehearsals for that one; we were on the set in North Carolina. We didn't rehearse everything; we rehearsed some complicated scenes. Holly Hunter likes to rehearse; she's an actor. Most directors, like Barry Levinson or Lasse Hallström, don't feel it's necessary to go through more than a few minutes of blocking: "You got the blocking down? Great!" Well, wait a minute. . . .

CZ: Do you ever demand more?

RD: Oh, yeah, sure. As a matter of fact, I've made sure of that; there were films where I said, "I'm demanding a week of rehearsal." But there are also directors who'll say, "Do it by yourself; I ain't gonna be there." There are also films that you don't need to rehearse; it's not like it's brain surgery.

Rehearsal, to a great extent, is used to create relaxation. You try to do it enough times so that you can relax and let something happen. You do it a hundred times, or fifty times; the more you do it, the better you're going to get at it. When you don't have rehearsal time, and you're doing it when the money clock is on, forget it. Your first instinct is going to be what's on film.

CZ: Was there ever any role where you said, "I can't get this. I really want someone to help me?"

RD: A lot. Especially once I became a celebrity—when no one helps you; they just think that you know how to do everything, or that whatever you do is O.K. A lot of thoughtlessness goes into making films and theater, as opposed to thoughtfulness. There have been times when I've said, "I'm at sea, here; I don't know what the hell I'm doing. I need some help."

CZ: There was a moment in Always *(1989) that was particularly moving. It's when you watch the character played by Brad Johnson kissing your former girlfriend, played by Holly Hunter, and you can't stand seeing it; you're close to tears. What kind of emotional preparation did you do for that? Do you get to that emotion by using the memory of a feeling or by using the given circumstance?*

RD: It's mostly circumstance. But you're an idiot if you don't try to remember when it really happened to you, so that you can recall that memory, that feeling. For the most part, I'm not an instinctual person, except when it comes to this, where I rely on my instincts more than thinking it through.

CZ: Do you look at dailies?

RD: It depends on the need. For instance, when I did *Stakeout*, I watched dailies every day, because I wanted to see what I was doing in relationship to the girl, and myself, and I'd never done a part like that. Sometimes I'll watch dailies or sometimes I'll watch a particular scene: "Did I do that right?" I neither stay away from dailies, nor am I attached to them.

CZ: In Rosencrantz and Guildenstern Are Dead *(1990), the use of language is nonnaturalistic, which makes it pretty different from your other roles. How did you deal with that kind of speech?*

RD: It was fun to deal with it: It's like Shakespeare. And it was fun to play another person. In my mind, I was playing Donald Wolfit, and I love that. There have been times when I played Spencer Tracy, and no one knew it, or I played Jimmy Cagney, and no one knew it; that time, I was playing Donald Wolfit. That's something I'd like to do again.

CZ: Why?

RD: Because I like doing it, and I'd like to do it better.

CZ: Do you usually feel that way?

RD: No, I don't. I'd like to play some of the character's attributes again. When I see *Rosencrantz*, I'm happy with this thing, but I could do better today; I could have done it better the Tuesday after. But it was a lot of fun.

CZ: What performances have been especially meaningful to you? And what do you think makes a great film actor?

RD: When I was growing up, there was a large group of actors that I loved. Tracy, Laughton, Brando, Stewart, Cagney, Grant, Fonda, all of them, the panoply of American and British actors. I used to watch all their films all of the time. I couldn't tell you how many times I have seen *Captain Blood* (1935), a hundred, at least. Each one of these actors offered me something different, something that I loved; that's why they were movie stars. Stardom is a love affair. It's a friendship and a love affair between the audience and the performer, and you love someone for a reason. There was no one more heroically graceful than Errol Flynn, never. Never was, never will be anyone who could make you believe in that myth as much as he could. He was beautiful and substantive in his beauty, and a far better actor than he or his contemporaries ever knew. Laughton was someone I listened to. I could listen to his voice and what he did with prose for hours. There was something unique about him; he could find a kind of rhythm in prose that no other actor has ever found as far as I know.

There's no one thing that makes a great film actor, because it is a mystery. There are great actors who aren't great film actors or great movie stars. There are great movie stars who are clearly not very good actors, yet somehow they are. I think there's a clear difference between celluloid and video and the stage. Celluloid helps to create a mysterious feeling, a kind of semi-religious experience that you can't articulate. Why is John Wayne great? And he is great. He was magnificent, and he was necessary. But was he a good actor? I don't know any more what that means. I used to say he wasn't, now I say he was. I think that *True Grit* (1969), *She Wore a Yellow Ribbon* (1949), and other performances of his are magnificent.

It's different in each person. Each person who becomes a film star speaks to something in people's hearts. Whether it's Kevin Costner, or Robert De Niro, or Jimmy Cagney, people are fulfilled by something, they recognize something, they want to see it again. Not everyone can do it; a person can look exactly like Jimmy Cagney and not have it. A person can act exactly like Kevin and not be Kevin. It's a chemical thing that is mysterious. It's not a measurable thing—this person's prose is better than that person's prose, or this person photographs better than that person. It has nothing to do with that; it has to do with a love affair. Why does a man fall in love with whomever he falls in love with? Why does a man leave a beautiful woman for an unattractive one? Why does an attractive woman fall in love with a nerdy little geek? Because it's mysterious, and it should be. Because there's something in his or her heart that is being fulfilled. Sometimes it's easier to equate—John Wayne fulfilled a massive American mythology. We needed it, and we still need it.

CZ: What do you think you personify?

RD: I don't know. I'm kind of in the eye of the hurricane; there's all this turbulence around me, and I'm in the eye of it. I have been told that I represent something about, like, the sixties, and going to college, and taking drugs, and the urban; that's who I am, somehow. I don't really know the answer to this question. I can't put on a mask and sit in an audience and listen to how people are responding to me; I just do the work. So far, no one has ever done a critique of the work of Richard Dreyfuss that I've ever read. One day, that might very well be done, and I'll learn something about myself.

CZ: Do you think film acting is historically bound?

RD: It can be, but it's not necessary that it be. I mean, why was Jimmy Cagney popular in Iowa and not only on the Lower East Side of New York? Because there was something about Jimmy Cagney that you couldn't take your eyes off. That's what charisma is; it can't be defined. If you can define it, it ain't charismatic. Why has James Dean remained popular? It's a mystery to me, I'll tell you that, but certainly not to three generations of people.

CZ: What about Brando?

RD: The gods came together on Marlon Brando. The gods came together and agreed to give this guy everything, because he not only had the most extraordinary intellectualized acting talent that I've ever run across, he had the courage to fulfill it, and he had the nobility of a lion and the grace of a panther; he had it all. Had he been an English actor, they would have named buildings after this guy. As it was, everything he achieved, he achieved against the opposition of a critical community that was incredibly ignorant, and so they turned him into a clown.

CZ: Don't you think he had a hand in that?

RD: In becoming a clown? Of course he did. We live in a culture that does not support—in the sense of intangible support—the art form that he was supreme in. What they said about him in *Julius Caesar* (1953), Hitler said about Poland. And when you look at it now, you see the most remarkable Shakespearean performance of that generation, and all the English actors knew it. Robert Shaw said it was an uncanny experience to have all these young English actors watching this American play Antony the way they'd always dreamed that it could be played. His imagination, his courage, his talent, his natural physical beauty, and his simple charisma—it's not so simple. You couldn't get any better than Marlon Brando. There was a period of ten years where everything he did was astonishingly good and courageous. Laurence Olivier, on the other hand, who is a great actor, is a great actor because of his courage, not because of his talent.

CZ: Can you talk more about that? I remember a remark by Peter Hall about the difference between Ralph Richardson and Laurence Olivier. He said that Richardson was an actor of genius and Olivier was a performer of genius. I thought that was an interesting distinction.

RD: I think that Laurence Olivier was the most courageous actor I've ever seen. And he was industrious, and industry is rare. I don't think his talent was great. A lot of his performances are kind of silly, but wow, did he eat them, and did he work, on a minute level, to make every moment of them complete. Some of his performances are magnificent, but he's known because he wasn't afraid.

Brando let it all go. Look at the culture that these two guys lived in. In one culture, Olivier was supported, propped up in his own pursuit of his career and his ambitions. In Brando's, he was left on his own. Everyone in America is left on their own.

CZ: There was a comment made not only by Brando, but also by Mickey Rourke in an interview, that acting is "women's work." Do you think that there are masculine and feminine vectors in emotion? Do you think that there are emotional constraints placed on you because of your gender?

RD: Of course; if you're going to show emotion, that's considered feminine. In England, there's less of that, because America is a kind of pioneer, frontier, rough-and-ready society.

But I think that acting can be described as inherently silly. One of the things that actors are always fighting against is the fact that they do in public what other people only do in private. There's something always embarrassing about acting, not only to actors, but to the audience. The essence of acting can be considered puerile: You are standing in front of people who are pretending they're not there; you are pretending that you are someone else, wearing clothes that aren't yours and saying lines that you're not thinking; I mean it's silly. And yet it's not. That's why Spencer Tracy, who I think is a fabulous film actor, also denigrated film acting and acting in general. I don't think acting is anything to be denigrated; to quote, it's not "women's work," it's man/woman's work, and you find your woman in you, and you find your man in you, and you do your job. I try not to sound like Tracy; Tracy meant a lot to me, and when I read the things that Tracy said, which were later said by Brando and Mickey

Rourke, I'm so disappointed. If I feel that coming out of me, I stop, because I don't want to mislead myself or anyone else. I try not to lay at the feet of acting what other disappointments or frustrations I may have.

CZ: You've said in an interview that "Nobody knows how to watch acting."
Can you address that?

RD: Because we don't consider acting a serious art form. But it is absolutely necessary, and without acting, people would simply drop dead on the streets. But people categorize actors, and, therefore, they don't have to critique them. When most people write about the work of Cagney, or Tracy, or whoever, they're just telling gossipy stories about their careers. They don't really watch what they do. Most times, people, when they watch movies, are so assaulted by other influences—music, and editing, and directing, and camera angle, and all that—that you don't know what you're getting from acting and what you're getting from the rest of it. That's O.K., there's nothing wrong with that. But that's why people find it difficult to watch acting, or to discern the difference between what the actor is actually doing and what they're receiving from the whole.

It's funny, when I was a young man and I used to sit around and bullshit about acting all night long, I had all these opinions about it; I don't have very many opinions about this any more. Acting is a fact as an art, and it will always be a fact. And if people have good or bad attitudes about it, it doesn't really matter. Because sooner or later, someone's going to write something, put it on film or stage, and hire actors. You've got to do that, or else you die, you wither away. Did you ever read a book called *Magic and Myth of the Movies*?

CZ: By Parker Tyler?

RD: Yeah. That is a wonderful book. It's the only book I've read that ever had the courage to say, "You want to know what going to a movie is all about? It's a religious experience, surrender to it, it's great." The first time you say that, people react, and then you carry them through it and they understand.

Someone who really minimized the power of acting, the most damaging influence to the American theatrical culture—and culture even in a larger sense—was Lee Strasberg. Because Lee Strasberg's personality was so powerful that he influenced not only a generation of actors, and succeeding generations, but succeeding generations of writers and directors. We are just coming out of a time, a good forty years, where Americans were taught that only a small portion of life was to be celebrated on stage, or in movies. There's an old story about what you had to do in order to be able to get into Shakespeare's Globe Theatre—you had to be an actor, a dancer, a mime, a juggler, a singer, and you had to play kings and peasants, princes and angels. None of this is demanded of us. After World War II, Lee Strasberg basically said, "No, you have to play just this narrow spectrum," and Stella Adler said, "No, it's not, it's bigger than that," and she was exiled. All of my generation suffer from this; I suffer from it. Bobby De Niro, who, in my opinion, is the finest actor of my generation and who could do almost anything, would be that much better had we not all been so terribly influenced by the restrictions put on us by Strasberg.

CZ: Do you mean the concentration on the rawness and reality of emotion?

RD: The concentration on the lower middle class and on emotional truth, as opposed to style and the rigors of discipline. I yearn, as a lazy person, for the rigor of discipline in my training, which I never had. In America they say, "Go out, sink or swim!" You can go to Carnegie or Yale, or you can get it on your own, but the culture itself doesn't demand the rigor of you. And that is, to a great extent, the pervasive influence of Strasberg. He didn't do this maliciously, but he did it, and we are suffering from it.

CZ: And yet there's someone like Kazan, who had largely the same way of thinking about acting as Strasberg and who is certainly responsible for some of the greatest film performances. For me, he's a great actors' director.

RD: Oh, and there are great actors from The Studio! But how much better would they have been, and what other movies would Kazan have made, had there been an acknowledgement that physical grace and style were demanded of us. I think that Kazan was a brilliant director and Strasberg was a great teacher, but Strasberg should have taught us about other things. Do you find that actors mostly like what they're doing?

CZ: Oh yes, absolutely.

RD: See, I find most actors say negative things. I would have liked to have known Tracy and asked him, "Do you really enjoy this? Come on Spencer." When I was younger, I had no friends who weren't actors. We used to sit around and talk about it, and one day, a girl that I knew said to me that she wished that another muse had chosen her. And I said, "You don't understand what acting is. Every art exists for a reason. Every art form does something to the human soul in a different way—dance, music, whatever it is. And acting is the only art form that does *that* [snaps fingers]." Music can affect you powerfully, and prose, and art, but no art form can make you burst into tears, or make you laugh by the immediate reflection of human behavior like acting can. And that's the nobility of acting, and that's why acting is feared, and that's why people are cautious about actors, and scared of them, and why they also want to elect them for president.

CZ: To me, that's why actors should be valued so much, because they're willing to go—as an acting coach said to me—into the depths of their soul, and come out again, and show people things about themselves.

RD: That's right. What actors can do without lecturing is show that in each of us there is Hitler and Jesus, and if you are a truly gifted actor, you can find that in you, and bring it out, and say, "See, we share this." For instance, a guy like Henry Fonda couldn't find Hitler in him; he was so lovable. There was this movie that he did once where he shot a whole family, and then ended up shooting this nine-year-old girl in the head, and you still didn't want to dislike him. One of the great things about certain actors is their ability to find that. De Niro can do that; he can be loved and hated. To find that is like going to church, except you don't have to stand and listen to the minister just say it to you. You can experience it, look at it, and say, "That's what I do. That's what I wish I could do. That's what I'm afraid of doing."

CZ: You've been acting in films for over twenty-five years. What's been the biggest surprise in your career?

RD: Life surprises you in a lot of ways. One of them is that I have this friend, this little nuclear pellet right here [touches chest], which engined my acting, my career, my ambition, my enthusiasm. Then one day, I realized that it had turned off, and I was filled with a kind of loneliness or despair about that, because it was so constant and had been with me my entire life. I didn't know what to do; I was at sixes and sevens. I realize I just have to adjust to what I am, and who I am now. In many ways, it'll make me a better actor in that I think *Tin Men* is a very good performance, and *Tin Men* is a performance that lacked that nuclear pellet; it was done in the absence of that. So was *Let It Ride*, so was *Stakeout*.

CZ: But you've gained a lot.

RD: At life, in the absence of that. But at the same time, there is an intimate relationship between me and it that isn't there any more. It's like if a marriage changes from love to friendship, or a friendship changes. You have to make that adjustment; that's what the last few years have been about. I'm now older, I have three children, and their welfare is infinitely more important to me than my acting is. My acting career is still important, but before, I was a single person who had nothing but this pursuit to interest him, and that's what I did, and that's what I loved. One day you wake up and you find there are all these other things you love now, and all these other interests.

The compulsion I worked under as a kid no longer exists, and I think my work will suffer from it, because I don't have the interest that I had. I have interest and affection, but I don't have the lust that I had.

Career Highlights

Film: *American Graffiti* (GGN) 73. *The Apprenticeship of Duddy Kravitz* 74. *Jaws* 75. *Close Encounters of the Third Kind* 77. *The Goodbye Girl*, (AA, BAFTA, GG) 77. *Whose Life Is It Anyway?* 81. *Down and Out in Beverly Hills* 86. *Nuts* (GGN) 87. *Tin Men* 87. *Stakeout* 87. *Always* 89. *Let It Ride* 89. *Once Around* 91. *Rosencrantz and Guildenstern Are Dead* 90. *Lost in Yonkers* 93. *Mr. Holland's Opus* (AAN, GGN) 95. *Night Falls on Manhattan* 97. *Cletis Tout* 2001.

Theater: *Whose Life Is It Anyway?* 79. *A Day in the Death of Joe Egg* 81. *Requiem for a Heavyweight* 83. *Incident at Vichy* 85. *Death and the Maiden* 92.

Television: *Lansky* 99. *Fail Safe* 2000. *The Day Reagan Was Shot* 2001. Series: "The Education of Max Bickford" 2001–present.

Tommy Lee Jones

*In acting . . . you use your creativity, your imagination, in
very real ways for a very specific job, and you go far and
wide to do that. And insofar as you get paid well and have a
chance to do the world some good, I'm really grateful for it.*

CAROLE ZUCKER: *You grew up in a small town in Texas. What was your
early experience of watching films?*

TOMMY LEE JONES: I grew up in extremely small towns up until the age of
six. The first movie I ever saw was at a movie house in the town of Rotan.
It was a double bill of an old Tarzan movie and a movie called *House of
Wax* (1953). It was a huge experience. It cost 25 cents, I believe: a dime
to get into the theater, a dime for popcorn, and a nickel for a Coke. I'd
been looking at this building in town whenever I was in town. I knew that
there was something going on, and I thought I had it pretty well figured
out until I got in there and a guy's face melted, and Tarzan was sur-
rounded by the pygmies in the tribe, and the big monkey tried to kill him.
It was a fantastic experience. I was a little old to be that naïve, probably
five or six years old.

I remember just that very day, I joined a baseball team—what you
would call Little League—and we'd all been given orange ball caps. I took
mine to the movie theater with me and got so badly scared that I bit the
little button off the top and was ashamed when I went to the baseball
diamond the next day that I had no button on top of my new ball cap.

CZ: Did you have any idols in the movies that you wanted to emulate?

TLJ: I thought Johnny Mack Brown was rather special. I didn't really see that anyone could aspire to be like Johnny Mack Brown; there couldn't be but one. I thought he was awesome.

CZ: When did you first think about becoming an actor? Where do you think that came from?

TLJ: I don't know. I don't suppose there's a turning point; I wanted to be an actor all my life. I was a very enthusiastic and quite histrionic back-yard foot soldier as a child. I enjoyed school plays, in the second and third grade, and thought it was a wonderful experience. It was scary. The world of the imagination appealed to me early on, but when I specifically decided to make my living with my imagination, I don't know.

CZ: Did you see any theater when you were growing up?

TLJ: I had never really seen any legitimate theatre other than little school plays, where you play a mole who's been blinded by the sun and held captive by the God of the Corn. Some pseudo-Native American myth, turned into a little school play. Or *Snow White and the Seven Dwarfs*, put on by the entire second grade of Rotan; I played Sneezy.

CZ: Were your parents supportive of your decision to become an actor?

TLJ: Yeah, sure, I suppose. Actually, they took me to see Lefty Frizell perform from the back of a flatbed truck, in a little knot of oak trees along the Concho River below San Angelo one time. I'll never forget that as long as I live; it was an amazing thing to see. I was taken to rodeos as a child. Town was always a big deal and a big surprise when I was a child. Speaking of theatrical events, going to town . . . that's probably when it started, when they took me to town [laughs]. It's a long way to answer your question, but that's it.

CZ: When you went to Harvard, did you take any theater classes?

TLJ: They don't have any; we're not a trade school. They had a legitimate theater company there, several of them. Lots of plays going on in a lot of colleges. Theater was a part of the undergraduate life in the late 1960s in Cambridge.

CZ: After you graduated, did you do repertory theater in the Boston area?

TLJ: That was my summer job. After I graduated, I went to work in New York, and worked in the theater.

CZ: Did you ever have any formal training as an actor?

TLJ: Well, I'd say my education as an actor has been entirely practical. Beginning at the age of sixteen, I started working on plays and did a minimum of three a year until I was twenty-four or twenty-five years old and working as a professional. I did a lot of classical plays in repertory and helped run theater companies, was in theater companies, acted in and directed plays constantly, for a long time, until I was too busy working in movies and television.

CZ: If you were talking to a young actor just starting out, would you recommend on-the-job training rather than acting classes?

TLJ: I'd say do what I did in this sense only: Cultivate your mind at every opportunity, and broaden your education. What do I mean by education? It's the classical concept of a liberal education—learn. The study of history, science, especially the English language, the history of art, the history of aesthetics, no small amount of religion. Study those things because they inform your work. It's the mind that will give your work any kind of breadth, scope, purpose, or service.

CZ: Do you make any distinction between the mind and the emotions?

TLJ: Oh, yeah—the heart, the mind. Of course you do, it's an old dichotomy. One informs the other in a properly balanced world, of course. The broader they are, the better actor you'll be. Pretty simple outlook. Of course, you do need all the practical experience you can get. Sooner or later, you're going to have to learn your way around a theater, how light works, how the process works, and how it can be manipulated to the greater good of the greatest number.

CZ: What kind of adjustment was it to go from theater to film?

TLJ: Well, you had to think about a lot of things and make the obvious adjustment, one that for some people is easiest to forget, which is the matter of scale. You'll find that actors who have a sense of scale in the theater will have an equally adept sense of scale before a camera. Those who cannot suit the action to the word and make too broad a gesture onstage are the same ones who are liable to jump out of frame in the middle of a good shot, or wave their hands in front of their face while they're wearing white gloves, or some other mistake.

CZ: What attracts you to a project?

TLJ: Well, people really. The person who wrote it, what he's done in the past, what kind of writer he is. The director, the company, and the people that make it up. The question is, "Do you want to make this movie with these people?" You really want to consider the people you're going to be working with; it's very important. Also, is it fun? Very important. [laughter] Fun is a highly underestimated thing in this country, especially in the arts.

CZ: Have you ever had a problem with a director because he approached the work differently than you did?

TLJ: The directors have all been different. So adaptability is important. A director told me one time that I couldn't watch dailies because I'd change my performance and would be out of control. I'd been making movies for a few years and made some really good ones at the time, and dailies were an important work tool. You'll find that people make up their minds ahead of time. Ordinarily, a person would find their intelligence insulted by such a thing. But you get over that and go on, you try to be adaptable. This is twentieth-century America, the audience is huge, these are important matters. You just go right by that kind of thing, go on to the next deal. You try to be adaptable, very, very, very important—key.

CZ: Once you're committed to doing a script, how do you develop your character?

TLJ: Well, you just read it! That's why it's important for actors to be good readers and to have had some kind of academic life where they're required to write a bit, essays and so forth, and organize their thinking. You just respond to the writing.

CZ: What kind of questions do you ask yourself when you read the script?

TLJ: How would a director respond to the writing? Will the director see the same thing in this that you do? Are you seeing it correctly? Are you working with people who appreciate what you see in it? Can you all become of a single mind and translate this literature into dramatic art or a commercial action adventure that's interesting in some way? Are these things possible? Those are the questions you ask yourself. I think training in literature is very helpful to an actor; it has been to me.

CZ: What excited you about the role of Gary Gilmore in The Executioner's Song *(1982)?*

TLJ: I'm a Norman Mailer fan, and have been all my reading life. He was very important to us in Cambridge, Massachusetts, in the 1960s, and continues to be important to me. His book, translated into his own teleplay, was irresistible—to be part of Norman's mental journey. I came to this as his *Crime and Punishment*. Having read the book and been in the play based on the book *Crime and Punishment*, it was a pretty good frame for huge dramatic events. And this was modern American art, with one of our great minds behind it. It was just awfully good company.

CZ: Did you do research into ex-cons and the Mormon community, that kind of thing?

TLJ: Yeah, sure. I had all the material available to me that Norman had available to him when he wrote the book. I had a collection of every magazine article and photograph that had ever been published of Gary, and every videotape interview—hours of tape, interviews with Gary and his family—and every foot of news footage. Everything there was. And I became good friends with his family. His cousin Sterling became a teamster, and I got him on as my driver. I lived in that little community.

CZ: How did you come to feel about Gary once you got into the part?

TLJ: They didn't kill him soon enough.

CZ: Both the series and the book seem to suggest that prison had warped him. What was your thinking about that?

TLJ: I think prison helped warp him. He wound up with no conscience, essentially. The movie shows how the conscience and crime and punishment are not as simple as we think they are. I'm sure if you go amongst the citizens and ask them if they would like to have a prison system that is rather brutal, offers no chance of rehabilitation, and will make a steady source of ever more highly educated criminals, they'd say, "No, we really don't want that." Most of them would be surprised if you were to say, "Well, that's what you have." These are not simple questions. We don't have a horrible prison system on purpose; it's very difficult. The strength and beauty and power in organized society is vulnerable; it's fragile. And it requires a lot of work to maintain it, by individual people and by society, even if it means killing somebody.

You could say he's a product of our prisons; it's true. The temptation is to say, "Well, okay, let's don't blame him. Let's don't kill him, let's let him live." The prosecution argued that it would cost a million dollars a year to keep him alive in maximum security—because of his prison record, not simply because of his shooting spree that one wild, drunken, stoned, crazy, idiot night. It would cost a million dollars a year to hold him, to keep him alive, and you still could not guarantee the safety of the other inmates around him, or the prison guards, or his own safety. That was the decisive argument.

CZ: When Gary kills the people, he does it in a very dispassionate way. Would you bring in biographical material as a way of understanding that?

TLJ: Yeah. He doesn't have much of a conscience. I think he probably had a delicate conscience to begin with; he didn't have a very happy childhood; he spent a lot of time in detention centers as a child; he rebelled against an unhappy family situation by stealing cars; he went to reform school.

CZ: Norman Mailer's book focuses on the big brouhaha going on with the media and on Gary demanding to be executed.

TLJ: Yeah, he enjoyed that; he was a real showboat, this guy. He loved that to death. Atrocious bullshit artist, this guy. Hurting people, doing something just horrible gave him a sense of well-being and achievement. Any atrocity did. Kind of a perverted outlook.

CZ: Do you find that you have to achieve some degree of empathy with a character, no matter how despicable he is? I'm thinking, again, of Gary, and also of your character in Stormy Monday *(1988), who really didn't have many redeeming features. Sometimes actors say, "I had to learn to love that character. Even though she was a person I would have hated in real life. I had to learn to love her in order to get inside of her."*

TLJ: You can't take a moral attitude toward these characters while you try to build a life for them. It shouldn't be a moral process. You're out there like a mad dog in a meat-house. You're not really thinking about what you like and don't like about certain characters; you're putting them together from your experience. That should be the only thing on your mind.

CZ: Is there anything that you wouldn't consider doing, because you were morally opposed to the character?

TLJ: No. I'm morally opposed to all bad guys, but you can't make a movie without a bad guy, whether you're the good guy or the bad guy. So what are you going to say, "I'm morally opposed to this character because he's evil"? You can say, "Oh, I don't like this movie because it admits of this evil, or it implies that this evil is greater than it really is, or it takes an attitude toward good and evil that I think is mistaken. I don't want to lend my efforts to this point of view of our world." You can take that hifalutin' posture, if you can afford it. Work should speak for itself.

CZ: You tend to play very intense characters; do you ever find that you take it home with you?

TLJ: No. A lot of young actors wind up doing that, but eventually you have to quit.

CZ: So you never had that problem, even at the beginning of your career in Jackson County Jail *(1976)?*

TLJ: I wasn't really a young actor; by the time I did that movie I'd been an actor for a good long time. I'd done twenty-five or thirty plays by then. I wasn't taking the character home with me as much as I did when I was a teenager. It's kind of an adolescent thing to do.

CZ: When you are in the process of doing a real-life character, and you've played a lot of them—Howard Hughes (The Amazing Howard Hughes, *1977), Doolittle* (Coal Miner's Daughter, *1980), Gary Gilmore, and Clay Shaw* (JFK, *1991)—how much did you feel the need to be faithful to the real person? How much imagination is involved?*

TLJ: Your first loyalty is to the man who signs your paycheck; then your loyalty is to the script and to the director and the work at hand. In some of those television shows and movies, it was important to the script that we create a convincing picture of what this person really was and really did, how they acted, even how they used their hands in certain circumstances, how they breathed—when they breathed in, when they breathed out. So you spend hours studying that, and you come up with a piece of film that looks astonishingly like RKO news footage from the 1920s, down to the patterns of speech and breath and details of clothing. So that's part of the style of the script. In other cases, that's not so important. It wasn't so important, for example, to be *the* Gary Gilmore, as it was to be *a* Gary Gilmore. The theme was crime and punishment, so I didn't look very much like Gary. Sometimes you need to try to look more like a historical figure than others.

CZ: Do you like to rehearse?

TLJ: Yeah! I do.

CZ: Have you ever wanted more rehearsal than you were able to get?

TLJ: Yes, I do! [laughter]

CZ: Some actors say they want to do it once and that's it; they can't stand rehearsing. Some people say it and, apparently, they don't mean it.

TLJ: Everybody I've heard say it didn't mean it.

CZ: Do you like to improvise? Have you ever been on a shoot where there's been a lot of improvisation asked of you?

TLJ: Look, I hate improvisation. I hate it. I don't mind planned accidents.

CZ: What would they be?

TLJ: There's a very subtle difference here, which I'm trying to figure out how to explain. [laughter] You can say, "Look, I want something to happen at this particular point in this little piece of literature." Somewhere, you can add a veil of spontaneity. How's that phrase? What I mean is something that seems uncontrolled, but isn't really. I don't like uncontrolled efforts.

I really feel that it's easy to abandon your narrative responsibilities when you are doing what most people would call improvising. I don't think anything unplanned has a significant place in any drama that purports to exist for the improvement of the time of good Americans.

CZ: Did you ever see a film with a lot of improvisation that's been interesting for you?

TJ: *McCabe & Mrs. Miller* (1971) was an interesting film; I liked the way it looked. Improvisation . . . I've made things up and put them on camera very shortly thereafter.

CZ: I notice that all your performances are very intensely physical. Your posture and your gestures are really different in every film. When people discuss acting they talk about working from the outside in or the inside out. Where would you be on that spectrum?

TLJ: I've heard this description before: This actor works from the outside in, that one works from the inside out. I've read interviews with actors who describe themselves accordingly, to be one way or the other. The influences on my work are wide, very wide. I find that's very important. So, I don't care if you go from the inside out or the outside in.

CZ: But physicality is obviously important to you.

TLJ: Hell, I want to get where I'm going; I don't care which way we go to get the character to seem real, to have the appearance of reality. You select those details of his behavior—mental, physical, emotional presence—that will inform the story and improve the time of the audience.

CZ: Mary Steenburgen said that she always gives an editor a place to cut a shot. Do you do that?

TLJ: That's one way an actor can control his performance, by creating cutting points. If you want to be a serviceable actor—which everyone should and has to be, if they're going to last—you do try to create cutting points in good and rightful places. Usually, you want to create about three, so the scene can be as short or as long as you need it to be. You can put cutting points in the middle of scenes; also, it depends on the relationship you have with the editor. That relationship is something in our industry that's getting closer. Most motion pictures are shot on location, so everybody doesn't go home at the end of the day; nobody has anything to do but work on the movie. These relationships naturally cultivate, and that's an important one to a healthy movie; the relationship between actor and editor. Please don't try these stunts in your own backyard, film students; these people are seasoned professionals.

It's not a socially facile thing; it's not an easy thing. When directors, actors, editors, and cinematographers are all working as a team, with lots of mutual respect, I think those are the ideal conditions. The whole point is that, yes, you do create editing points, good ones, but you don't want to overdo it. Read Hamlet's advice to the players; he tells you how to create a cutting point.

CZ: I wanted to go on to Lonesome Dove *(1989). Is the process any different when you have more screen time for your character to develop— eight hours as opposed to one and a half in a feature?*

TLJ: It wasn't much of a consideration. You have these events, the great arc of the story, and your character is here, here, here, and here, and you just play the character. It's a long journey. The fact that it was an eight-hour show really didn't effect any single decision.

CZ: Did you discuss the relationship among the characters with the other actors and director? I'm thinking especially about Gus and Call. Did you have discussions with Robert Duvall?

TLJ: I don't talk to Bobby a lot about anything other than football, or the weather, or to ridicule some young actor, or to tell jokes. I've known him a long time and have a close relationship with him; it really doesn't require a lot of talk to get down to work.

CZ: Did you use someone as a basis for the deportment of your character in that series?

TLJ: Oh yes, a collection of people. The book is a collection of ideas and jokes and fact and legend. All of it is centered around a place that happens to be my own place, Texas. I kind of built the character as a composite of several different people: the way one person used his hands, the way one person wore his hat or walked, especially around horses. I knew a man who was always tapping a horse between the eyes. The same thing applies to language and all the elements of character: moral outlook, and so forth.

CZ: Call is very well-dressed compared to all the other people in the film— he has pressed shirts, he's always well-groomed. Is that something you would bring to the characterization?

TLJ: Well, Woodrow's rather formal in his approach to life. Very perceptive on your part, keen observation.

CZ: Call and Gus, Robert Duvall, have a relationship that is very much like a marriage.

TLJ: Well, yeah, a close relationship, born of a place. Being out here, on horseback . . . all those years, chasing those bandits.

CZ: In the scene where Gus is dying, which is very moving, would you use the imaginary circumstance, or would you call on emotional memories of your own? You break down during that scene; you're obviously overcome with emotion.

TLJ: Actors call on emotional memory, that's what the job is.

CZ: People mean different things by emotional memory; they can be thinking about the death of their own father or brother, or something like that.

TLJ: Anything on heaven or earth, anything. The kitchen sink. So, the answer is probably yes.

CZ: As Clay Shaw in JFK, *you're very elegant, and erudite, and refined. It's very different from any other role that you've played. What kind of research did you do for the role of Clay Shaw? Did you study the gay milieu in New Orleans?*

TLJ: No. I interviewed Jim Garrison. What I wanted to understand first was Jim Garrison's understanding of Clay Shaw, so I sat with Jim for hours and hours, three two-hour interviews, and took notes and asked questions steadily, until he got too tired; he was sick. He explained at the beginning of the first interview that he could tell me more about Clay Shaw than Clay Shaw's mother could have ever told me. By the end of the six hours, I was convinced that he was right. I'd read a lot of books about Shaw. I kind of went around town and talked to different art gallery owners, retired attorneys, people on the street, and so forth. Then there were the endless volunteers with Clay Shaw stories.

One of the most useful sources was an interview two hours long with a man who worked for Clay Shaw: what kind of work they did, what he was like, and what he sounded like. I was told this man had an accent almost identical to Clay Shaw's. It was from this interview that I learned that he had painted himself up like the winged Mercury one Mardi Gras, and I went running, tape in hand, to Oliver Stone and said, "Got to paint myself in gold, man," and he said, "What?" I finally sold him on the idea. I would say that tape was the most useful thing, that tape and Jim. The main task at hand was to understand Jim's understanding, rather than to exhume Clay Shaw.

CZ: What do you feel has been your most difficult and challenging role? Has there ever been anything that really stumped you, where you said, "I don't know what this guy's about, I need help . . ."?

TLJ: Yeah. With a terrible screenplay based on a cheap book, with a stressed-out, overly burdened director, movies sometimes will get into a situation where it's one long series of more or less controlled wrecks and accidents. Pretty soon people begin to work not for the movie, but for survival. Their proper job description becomes guilt evasion/credit theft. Everybody, especially if they're young, will get confused at such a time, possibly even be so naïve as to go to a director and ask for help.

CZ: Why do you think that's naïve?

TLJ: Well, I'm being facetious. You're not supposed to need help; you're supposed to be help.

CZ: A lot of actors say directors are terrified of actors, that they'd rather be doing anything than talking to an actor.

TLJ: I would think so. As I think back, some are. I'm sure it's because a goodly number of actors seem to be such doofuses, such dingbats.

CZ: Maybe it's because directors are often people who need to control things, and actors are the one unpredictable element in their job.

TLJ: Oh, absolutely. What other kind of person would have that job? At some point, a director will have to turn an actor loose in front of a camera that's actually turned on, the actual lights up there. I'm sure Mike Ditka would rather be on the playing field, having fun. He'd want the same money, the same prestige, the same clothes, the same everything else that he's got now, but he'd still enjoy being out there on the field. He's gone to all that trouble to put that football team together, and has some twenty-one-year-old kid throw the damn ball? It should be Ditka out there playing quarterback. [laughs]

CZ: You're living in Texas, in San Antonio and on the ranch, and you're also working on films that are produced in Hollywood. Do you ever find that creates a conflict, or is it a dichotomy you deliberately have built into your life?

TLJ: I don't see it as a dichotomy. I don't see anything unusual about my life. Communication and transportation being what they are today, people can live anywhere they want to live, for the most part. I certainly can; my work doesn't require me to go to the same place every day, so I can live at home if I want to. I don't have to live next door to a motion picture or a television studio in Southern California, or next to a soap opera television studio in New York convenient to all those theaters. I did that for eight years. I can live anywhere I want; so I live at home, and I enjoy the cattle business. That's not an unusual thing. In acting, you travel a great deal, and you use your creativity, your imagination, in very real ways for a very specific job, and you go far and wide to do that. And insofar as you get paid well and have a chance to do the world some good, I'm really grateful for it. I don't see any dichotomies. I see more harmony than anything else.

Career Highlights

Film: *Coal Miner's Daughter* (GGN) 80. *The River Rat* 84. *Black Moon Rising* 86. *Stormy Monday* 88. *JFK* (AAN, BAFTAN) 91. *Under Seige* 92. *The Fugitive* (AA, BAFTAN, GG) 93. *Heaven and Earth* 93. *Blown Away* 94. *Blue Sky* 94. *The Client* 94. *Cobb* 94. *Natural Born Killers* 94. *Batman Forever* 95. *Men in Black* 97. *U.S. Marshals* 98. *Double Jeopardy* 99. *Rules of Engagement* 2000, *Space Cowboys* 2000. *The Hunted* 2001. *Men in Black 2* 2002.

Theater: *A Patriot for Me* 69. *Fortune and Men's Eyes* 69. *Four on a Garden* 71. *Ulysses in Nighttown* 74.

Television: *The Amazing Howard Hughes* 77. *The Executioner's Song* (Emmy) 82. *Lonesome Dove* (EmmyN, GGN) 89. *The Good Old Boys* (SAGN) 95.

Christine Lahti

*. . . that's the most exciting work I do, when I'm really scared.
I realized that those dark nights, those dark moments are
part of it; just as much a part of it as that feeling of exhilaration when you're flying.*

*CAROLE ZUCKER: When you came to New York from the University of
Michigan, you studied with Uta Hagen?*

CHRISTINE LAHTI: I adored Uta; she was a great teacher for me. She was really good, really supportive. I studied with her for two and a half years, and
then I went to Bill Esper from The Neighborhood Playhouse, who was really different. Had I to do it over again, I probably would go to Bill Esper
first, and then Uta, because Uta's so technical. She really helped me learn
how to score a scene—with objectives and actions, breaking down the
scene—whereas Bill really helped me learn how to use myself. His was a professional class, twice a week, for two years. The whole first year is improvisation. The training I got was really wonderful, and my own acting method is
a combination of many different teachers, but primarily Bill Esper and Uta.

CZ: What were you doing in New York in the meantime?

CL: Waitressing, waitressing, waitressing, and doing a ton of off-off-
Broadway plays, learning my craft. It was a great way to learn, actually
having the training and then being able to practice it, low stakes. I was
trying to get commercial agents—any kind of agents—it was really a
struggle. I pounded the pavement, like everybody else, stuck my picture

and resumé under doors, knocked on hundreds and hundreds of doors. Finally, my big break in theater was getting a part in *The Woods*, the David Mamet play that Ulu Grosbard directed.

CZ: Were your parents supportive of your decision to go into acting?

CL: Very, very much. The best gift they ever gave me was the feeling that I could do anything I set my mind to, which was amazing. So I had the confidence that I could do it, although there were many, many, many times when I felt like giving up, in New York, in the early days. I would be so discouraged and so frustrated, but something in me, some little voice hiding behind my pancreas or some organ in my body would say, "Keep going, keep going." There was something I needed to say—I need to say—with my work; sometimes it's political, sometimes it's just from my heart, or sometimes it's from my sense of humor. Whatever it is, there's a real need that I feel to act.

I think it's lessened now, since I had my children. When I didn't work before, I used to be really crazy. Early on, I would be completely without an identity when I didn't work; I didn't know who I was, I would feel empty. Recently, I went nine months without working; I was fine, because I have a very rich life now, with my kids, and my marriage. In the old days, if I had gone six months without working, I'd really be climbing the walls.

CZ: How did you get your first film role?

CL: Actually, my first role was in a TV film, *The Last Tenant* (1978), with Lee Strasberg and Tony LoBianco. I got . . . *And Justice For All* (1979) because Norman Jewison was watching *The Last Tenant*, for Lee Strasberg, and saw me, and asked about me. So it was one of those things.

CZ: When you look at your acting in . . . And Justice For All, *what do you see?*

CL: Now when I look at . . . *And Justice For All*, I see myself working too hard; I see myself trying to be charming, trying to be . . . just trying. And I don't think it was the character who was trying; I don't think there's a scene where the character was trying to charm somebody, or working a little hard. I think it was me just not trusting myself enough. Now, I've become simpler, and I trust myself more. I don't have to work as hard.

CZ: What makes you take a part? It probably isn't always up to you, but are there parts that you won't take or that you've turned down?

CL: It always has been up to me. I haven't really listened to anybody else; I've pretty much stuck with my own set of criteria, although I do ask people's advice. Mostly I look for variety; I look for different kinds of characters. I won't do—or I've tried not to do—anything that I find exploitive of women. I'm a feminist, and I'm so grateful to the women's movement, and feel so empowered by it. And being a feminist, to do any kind of part that is exploitive of women is completely objectionable to me. I've turned down many parts because of that; whether it was because the nudity was unnecessary and exploitive or that I felt the woman was primarily a two-dimensional sex object, an accessory. I'm not interested.

I have done, especially in my early days, parts that, on paper, read like two-dimensional sex objects, like my first television pilot. It was called *Dr. Scorpion* (1978), and I was a CIA agent. There were a lot of scenes written: "bikini-clad." I worked really hard with the director, and with my co-star, Nick Mancuso, to try to give this woman three dimensions and a sense of humor, and some vulnerability. I basically think I raised the level of it by a couple of notches, but it was still pretty tacky.

I've had to do certain things that I may not have otherwise done, because I needed money. But basically, I feel my integrity is intact. There's lots of different reasons to take jobs. And needs change; sometimes I just need to work, because it's been so long. Or the need for money —but my lifestyle's not that extravagant that I need to keep working all the time to support it. I've kept it that way on purpose, because I don't want to have to take stuff I don't believe in. It's important for me to feel passionate about what I do, and if I don't really have empathy, or a connection with the character, I don't know how to do it.

Other times you take it for the artistic challenge. I've often done parts that I had no idea how to do, but I've thought, "Mmmm, wouldn't it be neat if I could get this." That's happened a lot on stage; one that comes to mind is *Landscape of the Body*, the John Guare play. I had no clue how to do this lady, but it was such a great, exciting, scary experience. In *Housekeeping* (1987), the movie, I had no idea how to do the character of Sylvie. But I knew, in the back of my mind, that if I really took the chance, it might be something very exciting. I love parts like that, where I don't know what's going to happen, where they're going to end up.

CZ: You sound like you like a good challenge. Would you categorize yourself as a risk taker?

CL: Yeah. I think so; I'm an Aries. [laughter] Actually, that's the most exciting work that I do, when I'm really scared. I remember saying to my shrink, when I used to see one—usually, there'd be a dark night just before opening in a play, or a dark week during the filming of a movie or rehearsal—and I'd say to her, "I'm so scared, I think I'm going to fail, I don't know how to do this. . . ." And she'd say, "You know, you keep insisting on going way out on these limbs, and taking these chances, but what you don't get is that there's no safety net. If you take those chances, you may fall. You can't continue to challenge yourself and take these huge risks and expect there to be some safety net underneath—there's not. So if you go out there, that's the risk; you fall and pick yourself back up again, or you fly." That was a really great lesson; I realized that those dark nights, those dark moments are part of it; just as much a part of it as that feeling of exhilaration when you're flying.

CZ: Once you're committed to a project, what kind of research do you do? Do you create a biography and a backstory? How do you work with the directors of your films? The characters that I'm most interested in are Hazel in Swing Shift *(1984), Sylvie in* Housekeeping, *Annie in* Running on Empty *(1988), and Darly in* Leaving Normal *(1992).*

CL: You've picked my four favorites! Well, my own homework is the same regardless of the director I work with. First I go through the script, and I write down everything other people say about me, and all the clues about her history. Any clues about her parents, or birthplace or background, education. Then I fill in all the blanks with my own imagination. I follow an outline in terms of this biography, that I got from a book called *Writing a Screenplay.* It's really for a writer; it's an outline of a character, what you're supposed to cover in terms of background, physical appearance, psychology. The physical appearance is obvious, the background is in terms of parents, education, sisters and brothers, where you were born, place in the community, jobs, income, hobbies, interests, magazines you read, all that biographical stuff. The psychology is chief aspirations, dreams, goals, chief frustrations, obstacles, religion, whether the person is an optimist or a pessimist at the base of themselves. It's very specific, and I try to do it for every part.

Then I personalize everything, make it my own. Before I personalize everything, I try to think about objectives; I really score everything like Uta taught me. I think about what this character really wants in her life, scene by scene, in order to get this super-objective. In the script, I draw lines where the beat changes. It's very method; it's very Stanislavski. Then, for every scene, I think about actions, in terms of: What do you do to get what you want? Sometimes I think about what's in the way, the obstacle. But basically, it's to find behavior, which is really interesting to me.

CZ: Do you write all this down?

CL: Yeah, I do. Usually I fill out cards, because I'm shooting out of continuity. I fill out index cards with the scene number on it, what's just happened. What I do is create a literal arc with my cards, because if I'm shooting scene seventy-three on one day, and I want to know where I am emotionally in the arc of this character's growth, I grab scene seventy-three. I just have a general idea, and I look at the card, and I see the specifics.

Of course, it all changes in rehearsal; the ideal thing is that I do all this background stuff, break down every scene, and personalize everything, and then I try to forget everything I've done, and go on the set, or into rehearsal, and go from my gut. That was the problem with Uta, for me. Sometimes it remained in my head, it became so intellectual that it didn't really come out of my heart. So I do all that great work, which I find really fascinating. For example, with Hazel in *Swing Shift,* I saw a lot of documentaries about women during that time, during World War II, and *Rosie the Riveter* (1980), and read a lot of *Life* magazines for the period, and looked at pictures.

This is all work that sounds tedious, but I love it. The more I can enrich this character's life, the more alive I can make her. I create an arc for every character I do that is really specific. She starts at A and ends up at Z, or D, or . . . however big the arc is, however much the character changes. Usually it's about a journey of the character; it's like layers of an onion being removed. Layers of skin taken off until you get to the core of the person. What defenses does she start out with? What covers does she start out with? How does she lose them? And what does she lose to reveal—usually by the end, hopefully—a more honest, evolved person?

That was definitely true of Hazel; she was very guarded, and used humor a lot as a defense. She was a very lonely and insecure person underneath. So I plotted all that out as to how much I wanted to reveal in every scene, and what would make her more courageous about opening up to somebody. Now, Jonathan Demme works incredibly collaboratively, and he encouraged me to just try anything, which I love. I love being able to, again, take risks and try wild things. So, Hazel wants to prove that she's superior to everybody, especially people she knows are putting her down. At the beginning of the movie, Goldie Hawn's husband, Ed Harris, is ridiculing her, yelling at her: "Hey, you slut, turn down the music." What do I do to make myself more superior and act like I don't care what he says? Again, it's all behavior for me: What do you do to get what you want? *Do* is the operative word. If I shimmy at him as I'm walking by, it shows I'm completely impervious to his comments and couldn't give a shit about him. So that piece of behavior, the shimmy, I came up with as a way of getting what I want. I remember discussing this with Jonathan, and he loved it. Many times, I make a complete fool of myself, and I like that. If I'm in an atmosphere where the director is supportive of me and says pretty much anything goes, then I'm able to take the most risks, and I'm able to either come up with great stuff or make a fool of myself. Both things happen.

The dream thing is to do all that research and all that homework, and then forget it, go on the set, and work off the other person. That's really it, in a nutshell. And that's what I got from Esper: to put all your attention on the other person, which frees you from any self-consciousness. If you can really see what experience they're having—What's their face doing? What are they feeling?—that's truly listening and responding. That's the give and take, and the aliveness that I really value. I really am dependent on my fellow actors.

CZ: Let's talk more specifically about Sylvie in Housekeeping, *by Bill Forsyth.*

CL: With Sylvie, I had no idea who this character was. Diane Keaton was supposed to do it; she dropped out to do *Baby Boom* (1987). I met with Bill and I instantly knew that we would work well together, and he felt the same way. It's very interesting; I read the original book, thinking, "I'm gonna really get many clues into this mysterious character that Bill has written." Bill wrote a kind of skeleton, and I had to put flesh and blood, and muscles, and guts on her. I thought, "Well, I'll read the book and get a lot more." Well, I got some more, but, the truth is, the book and the script were written from a little girl's point of view, and Sylvie was such a mystery to this little girl that a lot of the blanks weren't filled in. So Bill and I had to fill them all in. I remember calling Bill up saying, "What does this character need? I can't play a character who doesn't need anything. It seems like she's above it all; she just floats through life like some kind of eccentric Auntie Mame character." He said "Oh, no," in this very thick Scottish brogue, which I barely understood, "Oh, no, there's stuff there, you know." Well, I had to find out; I had to create a much more complex character, and he encouraged that and helped me a lot. I had to find out what was wrong with her, what she needed. I decided that she was a drifter, a loner, an eccentric, because she had suffered so much abandonment in her life—she was left by so many people—and that in order to survive, she lived alone, like a hobo. She was fine with that, but that door of vulnerability, of intimacy, had been slammed shut.

CZ: Do you think that Sylvie regarded herself as lonely?

CL: She doesn't know she's lonely. It's not until she meets these little girls, Lucille and Ruthie, that, especially in Ruthie, she finds a kindred spirit, and the door that had been shut for years starts to open up a little bit, and she allows herself to get attached to these little girls. She finds herself needing them and loving them. But it's a real slow arc, a real slow evolution. It was interesting: Bill chose not to come in close; there were very few close-ups in the first half of the movie, because he wanted Sylvie to be mysterious. But I had to do all the work.

CZ: Sylvie has this great sense of wonder and childlikeness that hasn't been beaten out of her.

CL: She loves nature; she's incredibly in touch with that, and in touch with that childlike wonderment. Annie Dillard wrote this amazing book about nature, called *Pilgrim at Tinker Creek*; it so reminded me of the way Sylvie must look at a pond. If you ever want to know about a pond, and the bugs, and the algae, read that book; it's looking at a pond with the most childlike wonderment, but also with a knowledge of what everything is. So Sylvie—who I think is really bright, and has that wonderment—looks at nature this way. I re-read the book, and Annie Dillard wrote that she wanted to feel the curvature of the earth. Remember those long strides that Sylvie would take? That came out of Annie Dillard's book.

Some people, not too many, thought that Sylvie was a terrible influence on Ruthie, and that it was a tragic ending that Ruthie was going off with Sylvie. Did you think that?

CZ: No, I thought Sylvie was liberating her.

CL: Yeah, that's what I thought. But there were people who thought that Sylvie should have been locked up, she was so dangerous for this little girl. It was shocking when I heard this stuff, because I'd thought of Sylvie as one of the most incredible people, spirits, that I'd ever come across, and that she was liberating Ruthie from a life of rigid normalcy that would have killed her spirit.

CZ: Would you make up something about what had happened in her marriage that made her husband leave her?

CL: Oh, yeah. Everything I created in the background supported this idea of abandonment being the key issue for Sylvie. I thought maybe Sylvie took a job, and her husband was away in World War II, and when he came back, she had changed. She had become independent in a way that he couldn't handle. So there was a kind of feminist value issue going on. He left her, and it was a devastating blow. And her father died in a train wreck, so he was gone. She was incredibly close to her father. We improvised in rehearsal; Bill didn't know much about that, but we did it anyway, and I kind of taught the little girls about improvisation.

CZ: So I gather you're an actor who likes to rehearse and likes to improvise?

CL: Love it. I love rehearsal. There are some actors who feel that the more they rehearse, the less spontaneous they are. For me, it's the opposite: The more I rehearse, the more spontaneous I can be, the more I can explore and discover and reject certain choices. Then, on the day of shooting, I'm much more spontaneous, because I've got all this stuff that has secured me, that has planted me on the earth, that has given me a real life. Then, I can forget about it, and just play. Often I improvise on a scene that I don't understand in a deep way. If I just don't get it, I'll improvise with the other actor to try to figure out what I'm doing in the scene, what it is that I want in the scene. Using your own words and the same circumstances as the scene, you often find out what you're going after.

CZ: Did you ever work with a director who didn't want to rehearse, or where you couldn't rehearse because the cast couldn't get together until a few days before the shooting?

CL: That's horrifying to me. I think I've been really lucky; most directors I've worked with wanted to make me happy, and if they don't know much about rehearsal, they will rehearse because I want to. With Sidney Lumet, it was the most rehearsal I've ever had. He rehearses a film like a play; that was great.

CZ: How much did you relate to your character, Annie, in Running on Empty?

CL: In that film, I did a lot of research. Although I was in college during that time, and I was not as radical as Annie, I was certainly an activist. So I understood a lot of that period of time, and what that meant. Again, I created a whole biography on her: why she fell for this guy, what was wrong with her marriage. Annie was a person who, at the start of the film, was pretty numb, had pretty much given up, and found her passion again by the end of the movie.

I could relate to her in that what I feel as a feminist is often as passionate. Taking a stand as a woman on certain issues—for abortion, say—I tried to substitute those kinds of things that I feel really strongly about for Annie, in terms of her protesting the war back then.

CZ: Running on Empty *is a wonderful character study, and the ensemble work is really beautiful. I was wondering how Lumet talked with you, with the cast, about your various roles, how you felt about your son, and your husband. I didn't think that you loved him at all.*

CL: I think that the marriage had pretty much run out of gas, running on empty. The thing that united us now, at this point, was our flight, our escape, our being underground—and the kids. But yeah, I think you're right, as I recall, we had all kind of decided that the marriage wasn't great. He was older, he was the star radical, an Abbie Hoffman type of character on campus, and I had a more sheltered, wealthy background. He was so passionate and flamboyant and powerful. It was one of those relationships where he was my mentor and took me under his wing. And after fifteen years underground, it was like, "Please, enough already."

Annie's own potential was squelched because she was so young when she went underground, and became a mom early on, and was trying to do her best, raising kids in these circumstances. So her opportunity to be heroic, in a way, to do something that really mattered to somebody, was a chance that she grabbed. The opportunity to save her son, to release him, was not just about Annie or the kid, it was about her own need to do something, to realize her own potential. Why she married him probably had to do with her low self-esteem. Why do women glom on to these powerful, charismatic guys who probably aren't that good for them? Probably because of their own lack of self-worth.

CZ: He's also someone who's not like daddy. I mean, he's a Jewish "red-diaper" baby!

CL: Very different from daddy. So that was part of her own rebellion. The scene that everybody wants to talk about usually is the scene with my father. It's a wrenching scene, and it was written perfectly. Usually, I find that we change a lot of dialogue in scenes, but that scene we didn't touch. We didn't change one word, which is highly unusual in film. We didn't rehearse it too much either; I remember Sidney didn't want to, and I didn't want to. By the time we did it, I knew so much about Annie, and it was such an emotionally painful scene, that we didn't want to mess with it too much. Steven Hill was incredible. We all got the beat; we knew what we all wanted; we didn't have to improvise to find it.

We staged it a couple of times, and it was simple: two people in a restaurant. Sidney used two cameras that day, which was very helpful. It was so emotional that we didn't have to do it that many times—I think we did it five times. I knew that it was working when the entire crew was crying after the first take. We all looked around, Sidney and Steve and I looked around and these big burly guys from the union were wiping their eyes . . . it was really fun. *Running on Empty* is definitely my favorite film that I've done.

CZ: Have you noticed any similarities in the characters that you've chosen to play?

CL: Well, I think that Annie was kind of going through the motions of her life, and then she came into focus. It's something that's a recurring theme in my work, I find. Even Sylvie was going through the motions. She was fine, certainly; Annie's motions were much more anxious and troubled and fearful, but both were disengaged from their lives, from their spirits. Through the course of the film, they come into focus; they become in sync with their truest, most alive, open, and passionate selves, uncensored and unblocked.

I'm just realizing that is a pattern, because in *Leaving Normal,* I think that was also the case. Darly, who was really blocked, by the end of the movie found her truest voice again. She was going through the motions of her life, too, in a different way.

CZ: How do you find these characters in yourself? Do you believe that your life dovetails with your roles, and that you are shown things about yourself by the roles that you choose?

CL: With every part, every part. And it often happens in a part I've chosen to do; partly because of some change that I'm going through in my own life that I can identify with. I believe there are facets of almost everybody in us, that we're like prisms, and if you look deeply enough or hard enough, you can find those people inside of you. I think that all these characters are in me. Sylvie I had to really do some looking for; Darly in *Leaving Normal* is closer to me in a way, but then Darly was the most covered up, the darkest character I've ever played. By *darkness,* I mean "hidden," obscure, dark secrets. Darly's not so sad, she's dark in that she's so mysterious, and has this kind of self-loathing.

CZ: That performance was so different than anything you've done, because it's so bold and brassy and loud and vulgar. It must have been really fun to do.

CL: It was so fun. I got to fly for that part, and I just loved it. She was outrageous, and again, Ed Zwick loves rehearsal. We did a lot of improvisation. There was one time, I remember, Meg Tilly and I were working on this scene where we're having a contest about who's done the worst things in our lives. We were doing it, and it wasn't costing enough. So Ed suggested this great improv where it's Meg and Christine, revealing the worst things we've ever done to someone; it was so personal. We both revealed this horrible stuff, and, of course, that is exactly what these two characters are doing. It's dangerous stuff to play with, but it was successful because it allowed Meg and I to trust each other in a way that we hadn't. It allowed both of us to feel the kind of closeness these two characters finally do feel.

CZ: I thought the script for Leaving Normal *was really good.*

CL: Me too. I loved that script, and I loved the making of that movie; I loved everything about it except how it was released and how the critics compared it—very unfairly, I thought—to *Thelma & Louise* (1991).

CZ: Well, it's about two women in a car.

CL: That's where it stops. Mostly male critics dismissed it as a second-rate *Thelma & Louise.* Had they reviewed it as a film on its own terms and didn't like it, that's fine, but to review it in comparison to this other thing . . . they were really apples and oranges. On the surface, yeah, there were a lot of similarities, but the journeys of these women were completely different. The focus of our movie was on the friendship. There was no action, and there was no violence.

The part that was really disappointing to me was that I felt like *Thelma & Louise* was the beginning, opening some doors for other movies about women. And instead, it seemed like it closed doors, for some critics. *Thelma & Louise* was popular; it was received well critically and at the box office. That makes it all the better for us, because people will want to see movies about women. The studio will support it: "Well, this movie made a lot of money, maybe this one. . . ." Instead, it was the opposite, "Well, you women, you had your shot at a female buddy movie, and no more." So, basically, the studio dumped it.

CZ: That must be really upsetting.

CL: It was. I think it's some of my best work. It was a wonderful movie for me, and Meg, and such a departure for Ed Zwick, after *Glory* (1989). It was a small movie that didn't have any action and violence and sex, so it had to be handled in a special way.

CZ: Have you ever worked with actors who you feel weren't doing their homework?

CL: Oh, yeah.

CZ: Does that piss you off?

CL: Yeah, it does. I've been lucky that I've worked with some great, great people, but there have been times where I've felt that people are making choices that were way off circumstances, and don't make any sense, because they want to be charming or sexy in a scene, or they want people to like them; they make completely weird choices that have nothing to do with the character. They're more personality-type actors than character actors, people who just use their own personalities.

CZ: A lot of actors have told me that directors are terrified of actors and don't want to deal with them.

CL: Well, I've only worked with two directors—who shall remain nameless—who were afraid of me. And that fear manifested itself in a kind of indifference or a kind of condescension. But basically, I think, it was that they were afraid of the intimacy and openness with which I like to work. I demand a lot from a director; I bring a lot of stuff to the table, a lot of ideas. A lot of them suck, and a few of them are really good. The directors who are able to listen, and able to say, "I don't know," are my kind of directors. The directors who have a quick yes or no response, I don't want to work with. It's the directors who are the most secure who are able to say, "I don't know. You tell me. Let's explore. That sounds good; let's try that." The ones who are insecure will say, "Oh, no, no, that's not going to work. No, no. The way this has to be done is. . . ." I don't want to work with them.

CZ: Do you feel your work on stage and film is different? Do you tone down or bring it up?

CL: Truthfully, I don't make any adjustments between stage and film; they're the same exact thing for me. The only slight thing I might do, depending on the theater, is project a little bit more. That's it. I don't tone anything down, or tone anything up, or change my body. Some people say, "Well, what about for close-ups?" No! I don't change my face; I don't think about what my face is doing. My face is my face, and if I'm telling the truth, it's going to be alive, it's going to be honest. If I think about my face, then I'm not in the scene. I'm not in the scene if I'm thinking, "Well, I have to keep my face kind of calm and expressionless, because the camera's so close, and after a bit I should go [screech]!" If the look on my face is ugly, I don't care; it's not my concern.

Now, before the camera's rolling, I've learned to become aware of lighting and things like that, because it is a very visual medium, and I'm learning that it's an important thing. And makeup is important; how I look is important. But while the cameras are rolling, if I think for a moment about how I'm looking, I'm not there. As Bill Esper used to say, "A mirror is the worst enemy of an actor." Self-consciousness. If you are thinking about yourself and what you're looking like, you're not in the scene. I'm really just saying the old Jimmy Cagney thing, "Plant both feet on the ground, say your lines, and tell the truth."

CZ: How do you feel about fame?

CL: Well, I don't feel that I'm that famous, so it's not that big a problem. The amount of fame I have, frankly, is kind of nice. It's not too intrusive—it's not like every time I go to a restaurant, I'm stared at. Sometimes it makes me uncomfortable, and a lot of times it makes me feel good when people—not when they stare at me or intrude—but if they come up to me on the street or in a store and say, "I love your work" or "I loved this movie." That makes me feel good. It's not gotten to the point where I imagine it is like for Julia Roberts, who is just inundated, who has no privacy. I have a lot of privacy, and I think if it ever got to the point where I was like a Tom Cruise or something—I doubt that's ever going to happen to me—if I was that mainstream a success, it would be horrible. I don't know how those people deal with it. But the amount of fame I have in my life now is nice; it's fine.

Career Highlights

Film: . . . *And Justice for All* 79. *Whose Life Is It Anyway?* 81. *Swing Shift* (New York Film Critics Circle, AAN, GGN) 84. *Housekeeping* 87. *Running on Empty* (Los Angeles Film Critics Award) 88. *Leaving Normal* 92. *Leiberman in Love* (AA for direction, live action, short film) 95. *My First Mister* 2001 (director).

Theater: *The Woods* 78. *Division Street* 80. *Loose Ends* 81. *Present Laughter* 83. *The Country Girl* 84. *Landscape of the Body* 84. *Cat on a Hot Tin Roof* 85. *Little Murders* 87. *The Heidi Chronicles* 89. *Three Hotels* 93.

Television: *The Last Tenant* 78. *The Executioner's Song* 82. *Amerika* (GGN) 87. *No Place Like Home* (GG, EmmyN) 89. *Crazy From the Heart* 91. *Judgment Day: The Ellie Nesler Story* 99. *An American Daughter* (GGN) 2000. Series: "Chicago Hope" (GG, Emmy) 95–99.

John Lithgow

People like to see the exuberance of my acting. . . . There have been very few roles that I've done quietly and modestly.

CAROLE ZUCKER: *When did you first know that you wanted to be an actor? You seem to have started acting at a very young age.*

JOHN LITHGOW: Well, I'll give you my little capsule biography, because it sort of answers that question. I grew up in a theater family—my dad began as an academic, although he always acted and directed. In Yellow Springs, Ohio, when he was teaching at Antioch, he devised a summer Shakespeare festival back in 1951, which became the model for his own work for the next thirty years. He was a producer of regional theater repertory. So I grew up with it; I was only six years old the first summer of this festival.

CZ: Did you grow up in Yellow Springs?

JL: Yeah. Until I was about ten, and then we started a very gypsy-like life, because my father went from place to place, always doing theater work. So I grew up very much of the theater, did a lot of acting for the fun of it, as an extra or a bit-part player in my dad's Shakespeare festivals, and did not really intend to be an actor. In a way, being that close to it, I wanted to avoid it. I was much more interested in painting—that was always the thing. If anybody ever asked me, "What are you going to be when you grow up?" I would say, "An artist."

By the time I graduated high school, I was still very serious about art, studying at the Art Student's League on Saturday mornings, commuting from Princeton, New Jersey, where we had ended up, and working very seriously in charcoal and watercolor, and doing printmaking pretty seriously. Then I went off to Harvard. If anybody asks me, "Why did you go to Harvard if you wanted to be an artist?" I always say, "Because I got in." If Harvard beckons, you follow. It seemed like a very exciting place to go; I was very pleased to have gotten in, and also they had this brand new and beautiful visual arts center, The Carpenter Center, so I thought, "Oh, good, I'll be able to do art."

CZ: What year did you start at Harvard?

JL: I arrived in sixty-three. Once at Harvard, first of all I discovered that there wasn't much of a program for painting, nor for any of the other creative arts, academically, at Harvard. Naïvely, I didn't really bother to discover that before I went.

CZ: There was no theater program at Harvard, right? What did you study?

JL: English History and Literature. But the extracurricular theater was so vibrant and exciting, and I fell into it so quickly, and was so good at it that I was immediately hailed as the big new actor on campus. Even as a freshman, I got the lead in one of the main stage shows. I would say that by the end of my sophomore year, I had decided pretty much to be an actor. By that time, I had done seven or eight different roles. I had even started directing at Harvard. So I just felt like I was destined to be a man of the theater. I always thought of it as repertory theater, very much in my father's mold.

CZ: Were your parents supportive of your decision?

JL: They were worried. I find myself, right now, exactly where my parents were at when I was graduating from Harvard. My son is going to be an actor, and I'm quite nervous about it because I know what's involved. The good news is he knows too!

CZ: You then went to London to study; why did you want to be in England?

JL: I wanted to go overseas. I got a Fulbright in my senior year to go to London and study acting in earnest at the London Academy of Music and Dramatic Art. Back in those days, and I think still, the Fulbright Committee places two acting students at LAMDA in their one-year program.

I was infatuated with British theater, and that was a very good time for it. Peter Brook and Peter Hall and Trevor Nunn were all at the height of their powers, doing great things, and there were a lot of great actors at work, and, as I say, I had grown up very much a repertory and Shakespearean actor. So I was very drawn to England.

CZ: Can you describe what the training was like at LAMDA?

JL: It was very, very rigorous and academic. We arrived at nine in the morning, and we were there until five or six every day. The morning was devoted to various technical aspects of acting: voice, diction, movement, historic dance, fight arranging, tumbling, all sorts of things, a very detailed schedule. The afternoons were devoted to rehearsals for two-month-long projects. Over the course of the year, we did about four or five plays. I extended my Fulbright a second year, and worked as an assistant director and basically a kind of production assistant and intern at the RSC [Royal Shakespeare Company].

CZ: That must have been exciting.

JL: It was great. I was also trying to stay out of the U.S. Army by prolonging my graduate studies abroad. That was certainly an element.

CZ: It's time for the classic question—do you see a big difference between British and American actors?

JL: Yes, I think there is a difference. It's a very complicated relationship between the British actor and the American actor. There's a kind of mutual envy, curiously enough, and a mutual inferiority complex. American actors tend to think the Brits are the great stage actors, and the Brits tend to think the Americans are the ones who act truly from the guts. A lot of them don't like to feel that way, but they do. I myself am such a hybrid, because of having grown up in the tiny little American repertory theater system and having studied in England. I really can move back and forth between two different schools.

CZ: How would you characterize those two schools? You have British training—do you see a difference between yourself and people who came from, for example, The Actors Studio and The Neighborhood Playhouse?

JL: I do think there's a difference. It's very much a difference in approach, and there's nothing preventing us from acting very well together. At its most rudimentary, it's the difference between acting from the outside in and acting from the inside out—the outside in being the British system. I do it both ways: I act from the inside and the outside simultaneously, my own hybrid. Also, every actor has to act according to the project and the material and the director. Every job is so different and the demands made on you are so different, you have to be able to work according to many peoples' methods.

CZ: Do you ever find it a problem to get in synch with people who have different training than you?

JL: Sometimes, but quite rarely. I've acted with a few actors who take acting far more seriously, if not grimly, than I do. I mean, I take it plenty seriously, but I'm also very playful about acting.

CZ: How does it manifest itself when people take it grimly?

JL: Just a different rhythm of working, a different tone. You really run up against tough problems with actors who are very insecure, and think that they have to totally be whatever they need to be that day. As a result, you can't enter their world, they close you out, they exclude you.

CZ: That sounds like the standard complaint about actors from The Actors Studio, that they can be self-centered.

JL: Yeah. Certainly it works great for some people, but . . . . I would say it's only been a problem with me maybe twice in a hundred jobs. All actors are insecure, and insecurity manifests itself in many ways.

CZ: Let's move on to your career in films. How did you get your first part? Was it in Dealing, *or* The Berkeley-to-Boston Forty-Brick Lost-Bag Blues, *(1972)?*

JL: Yes, exactly. It was about dope-dealing at Harvard. Somebody recommended me to Paul Williams, who said, "Oh yeah, John Lithgow, he used to act at the Loeb Theater Center at Harvard," so I got myself a great big movie part in a Warner Brothers picture. I never thought I would be in movies, and here I was acting in a movie.

CZ: What was the transition to film like for a stage actor? How did you feel when you saw yourself for the first time on the screen?

JL: I hated the sight of myself; it absolutely made me cringe. I think the main challenge was restraint. When you grow up in the theater, especially in the rep theater, you tend to think you're not doing your job if you're not acting your head off. Many directors early on told me, "Keep it more contained; you don't have to do so much, just think it." I worked with a lovely man named Robert M. Young in a film called *Rich Kids* (1979). There was a very key day, when I was confronted by my daughter in the midst of a divorce; it's a harrowing scene, and I was all ready to tear a passion to tatters, and he said to me, "Just do nothing." The nice scenes in that film are those scenes, where there's huge emotion going on, and we made a deliberate choice to play against it. There's a lovely scene where I'm moving out of the apartment, and there's small talk with my wife about what I've left and what I've taken; it's a very prosaic scene, but it's very touching. Bruce Beresford has been like that with me, just containing my work a little bit. It's always an issue, because I will always come in strong and then let the director take it down. I will even tell them I'm going to do it; I'll say, "Let me do it big, and you tell me how you want me to modulate it." Unless they see the full extent of it, they're not going to know what they have here.

CZ: So you think it's the director's job to take it down for you?

JL: Oh, yeah. I encourage them; I say, "I'll overdo this given half a chance, so you make sure you keep an eye on me." There's no reason not to put that right on the table. There have been very few roles that I've done quietly and modestly. I'm always looking for them, and very often I start out intending to play something quietly and it just gets bigger and bigger as we go along!

CZ: Were you a film buff in college?

JL: Oh, sure. I loved films. My Harvard roommate was consumed with films—David Ansen, who's now a *Newsweek* film critic. We used to go to films all the time; he was my film education. You know, Harvard Square was such a great place for movies back in those days, in Boston.

CZ: Did you ever study film performances in order to act in a film yourself?

JL: No, I never have.

CZ: The reason I ask is because I was watching Buckaroo Banzai *(1984), and your performance of Emilio Lizardo seems very influenced by German Expressionist film.*

JL: Yes, I know, I remember it being compared to *The Cabinet of Dr. Caligari* (1919). I did see *Caligari* as an undergraduate at Harvard—with Ansen, in fact. I don't know, I have a sort of huge backlog of disorganized memories and impressions that I draw from. I remember quite consciously, in the case of *Buckaroo Banzai*, working from an image of Mussolini.

CZ: I was thinking of Brecht's play Arturo Ui *also, as I was watching you.*

JL: Yeah. That speech to the crowd is very much Arturo Ui. A blend of Leonard Rossiter, the British actor, as Arturo Ui and Mussolini, but not very consciously.

CZ: I'd like you to take me through a specific role you've done, and tell me how you work on the character from its inception.

JL: In the case of Roberta Muldoon in *The World According to Garp* (1982), which is certainly one of my more "noted" performances, the most "out there," we had endless costume fittings, which were necessary anyway, but the costume fittings and the hair and makeup tests were in themselves a wonderful way of building the character. I began to see the character visually take shape before my eyes, standing for two hours having basically a body fitted on me, and experimenting with the size of the breasts and hips and different pieces of clothing. Ann Roth is a brilliant costumer. We would summon up pictures for each other, you know, who Roberta would look like. We hit on a young Julia Child, which is what she ended up looking like.

I realized that I had done a lot of unwitting research on Roberta Muldoon years before when, purely out of curiosity, I had read a book by Jan Morris, called *Conundrum,* which was her memoir of the transition from being a male to a female. I remembered watching her on Dick Cavett and one or two other talk shows, and being fascinated by her just as a person, never knowing that I would play a transsexual. She seemed captivating, and what she'd been through seemed like a fascinating transformation. You know, a sort of Tiresias person, who has seen life as both a male and a female. There was something magical about her, which just captured my fancy, and there I was, about five or six years later, playing a transsexual, and remembering her, and summoning up the memory of her extraordinary self-possession and sense of irony about herself and peoples' response to what she'd done. It was a piece of unwitting research, and in a way, it makes me think that I'm doing research all the time, just by being curious about people, and about life. Getting into that character was a very long and elaborate process. We worked with the director George Roy Hill, who rehearsed that movie very much as you would rehearse a play, for two solid weeks.

CZ: That's unusual.

JL: Very unusual for a film, but very necessary for me. The interesting thing was I rehearsed it as a man; I didn't even wear a skirt, or anything. It was very important to me that everybody got accustomed to me physically, acting that character, that I get very comfortable with Robin Williams, for example. Hugging and being very physical with him, selecting very carefully the moments when I would actually kiss him. There are three kisses, just affectionate kisses between a male and a female friend. Getting to the point where we were so easy with it that it was no longer a joke.

That's a very extreme example of something that you always have to go through—you have to get people accustomed to you in character. There's always a fascinating tension between the person and the character he's playing, sort of a hybrid that's invented, in between, and people to get accustomed to that hybrid and respond to it. Very often, that process has to happen quickly, because often you're doing a movie with no rehearsal at all. So you have to be at peace with yourself and banish your own insecurities as fast as you can, in a way, to disarm the people you're working with.

CZ: You're an actor who likes rehearsal, right?

JL: Yeah, I do like rehearsal, and if we're not getting any rehearsal at all, I will tend to say, "Well, can we just run this once? Can we just run it in front of the camera? Can I do it one more time before we shoot?"

CZ: Do you find directors are responsive to those requests?

JL: Oh yeah, because it's a very exciting process. You will work with many people in the movies who have never rehearsed; it's not part of their process. They just turn up and turn in what they're hired for, what people are familiar with.

CZ: Some directors don't believe in rehearsal for film, because they feel actors lose their spontaneity.

JL: There's a degree of that, but I've worked with some actors who I think take it to an extreme. I'm sure those directors want actors to know exactly what they're doing in the course of a shot. He'll want them to know where to hit the mark, and which way they're going to turn, and how they're going to deal with a prop, and how to keep everything in continuity, from angle to angle.

I'll tell you what's fascinating—in theater, you spend four weeks getting a moment exactly right. In shooting a film, you're shooting the process of discovering that moment, and you want to capture the process. Very often in rehearsing a play, you'll find a moment which is absolutely magic after only ten days. If it's supposed to be funny, it'll be hilarious; if it's supposed to be moving, everybody will be sobbing. But that moment will be gone after another three weeks of rehearsal, and then you go into the very difficult process of getting it back to the point where you can do it and make it fresh for a new audience every night, and recall the fact that it may be the hundredth time for you, but it's the first time for the audience. In movies, what the director is after is that magical moment ten days into theater rehearsal—that moment of first discovery.

But I've been through it as an actor—getting the moment perfect and then losing it, losing the life of it. On movies, you try to carefully monitor the progress of a scene in the course of a day, so that you're reaching the right moment just when you need it most, in a close-up or in the vital two-shot. My own philosophy is "Get it great in every angle," so that the directors can do whatever they want with the shots. But at heart, you are constantly recalling, "Keep this fresh; remember you'll still be doing the same moment three hours from now; make sure you have it right."

CZ: Do you find that you are given the latitude to improvise when you're working on films?

JL: Sometimes. Again, it depends. There are some control freaks, and some people who love the freshness of improvisation. It's very rare that you improvise on film, because, as I say, you've got to match everything. But it's a pretty good tool for discovering the essence of the scene. There's an awful lot of talk on a film set, usually, just analyzing what's going on.

CZ: Have you found directors to be very helpful in that analysis?

JL: Some. Theater directors are much more helpful than film directors are, because film directors have much more on their minds than just the interplay of the actors. Some film directors I've worked with say, "I don't even know how to rehearse. I never know what to do in rehearsal." You'd be surprised at how often that's the case. They say, "Well, what'll we do? Shall we read the script? What do you think? What would you like to do?" "You call it, you're the coach. . . . "

CZ: A few people I've interviewed have said that there's a war going on between directors and actors, and that directors are often terrified of actors and actors' questions. Have you found that to be true?

JL: I don't think it's a war, but it's probably another theme you've hit on: Actors are very insecure, they're worried about a hundred things, and directors don't have time for all those worries. They can get very impatient, and I don't blame them. I know what I put some directors through. You know, the good ones are forebearing and patient, or if they think an actor needs a little pushing, they'll go ahead and give a push, and they'll have the correct manners when doing it. They will have done it often enough to know what works and what doesn't, what shuts an actor down and what opens him up. Believe me, there are all varieties of experience in this relationship.

CZ: I was watching At Play in the Fields of the Lord *(1991) and wondering what happens when an actor you work with is less experienced than you? It struck me, as I was watching your scenes with Daryl Hannah, that you were very unevenly matched in terms of your talent. I found it very disconcerting.*

JL: Well, Daryl and I are very different actors, of course. Daryl is accustomed to being a "movie star," and a very girlish one. That's her great strength; her wonderful performances are in movies like *Splash* (1984) where she is kind of an innocent who has stumbled into someone else's world. Perhaps Daryl and I were mismatched in all sorts of ways. I tend to fault the director when that happens. I think that *At Play in the Fields of the Lord* had all sorts of problems. We were not brought into an ensemble. I think it happened in the casting, but I think it also happened in the making of the movie, and, ultimately, it happened in the cutting of the movie. The movie was six hours long when it was cut together, and they had to cut it in half, and they took all the mortar out of it. It was a very disjointed film in terms of the relationship of those five or six principal characters.

CZ: Aidan Quinn in that film gives an archetypal example of an "inside-out" performance.

JL: It's funny, because Aidan is a very good friend of mine, and we actually had a wonderful time working together, but he and I are from completely different schools. When people ask me, "Have you worked with actors who don't like to rehearse?" Aidan is always the one I think of first. He really does believe that a performance is ruined by over-rehearsing it. It was an enormous explosion on the set of *At Play in the Fields*, because the director, Hector Babenco, was making us do a scene too often, because he couldn't figure out how to shoot it. Aidan said, "I'm losing it, I will not be able to play this scene if I do it any more." I never have that problem. On the other hand, I think Aidan really is capable of finding the freshness of a moment better than I am. He is less technical. It's very interesting, because Aidan and I admired each other in many ways for exactly what we felt we were incapable of doing. He and I are polar opposites in many ways, but we really learned a lot from each other. I think from me, Aidan learned to enjoy himself a little bit more. From him, I learned an awful lot about concentration and restraint. He thought I was overdoing certain moments, and then I saw the movie and I saw that he was right. I mean, I come not only from the theater, but from classic theater, and from rep theater, in which an awful lot of wretched excesses and bad habits can grow up.

CZ: Do you find that you watch dailies a lot?

JL: I've started to a little bit more. There was a long period when I didn't watch dailies at all. I never watched them during *At Play in the Fields*, and off went Aidan every single night and studied them in great detail. Mainly, I'm not very comfortable looking at myself acting. I like seeing the movies, but watching dailies is sort of a no win situation. If you hate what you're doing, you can't get them to reshoot it, and if you love what you're doing, chances are they'll cut it out! So you end up frustrated anyway. I used to have this kind of theoretical rationale that looking at yourself acting, scrutinizing yourself, only constrains you. I don't really think that's true any more. I basically thought it was boring, and at the end of the day, I didn't want to go through it. I'd rather go to supper than go to dailies! I'm a little ill at ease; it's an odd situation where everybody's sitting around watching you, and you hope they'll laugh and they don't laugh, or they make no comment whatever, in which case your immediate reaction is "Oh, I was terrible," when in fact all they were looking at was the focus and the light and the sound.

CZ: You've mentioned the word excess *a few times. Do you see it as a positive quality to your acting?*

JL: Yeah, sure. I do believe that you get a sense of what you're good at and what people like about your work, and I think, in my case, people like to see the exuberance of my acting. It's not to everybody's taste, and sometimes I overdo it and people can't stand it. I think my performances in *The Twilight Zone* (1983), and *Buckaroo Banzai*, and a couple of other things are so extravagant that people kind of dig that; they'll sort of wait for what I'm going to do next. On the other hand, I think it's probably a relief for those people who are paying attention when I do something like *Terms of Endearment* (1983), which is very quiet.

CZ: That's one of the few roles you've had where you get to have a romance. Do you feel like you missed out in not getting romantic leads?

JL: Oh, no. I have a pretty good sense of who I am as an actor, and I think I'm sort of appealing without being the stuff of romance. I'm a little bit uncomfortable playing romance, myself.

CZ: Why?

JL: I don't know. Probably because I haven't been in that role very often. It could be because it's too close to home. I feel liberated by playing a role very unlike myself, and romance really is unleashing your own personality and feelings and putting it into play. And I think I'm a little odd for a romantic lead; I'm a little subversive as an actor. And, you know, because nobody's ever thought of me in that vein, I've never acted in that vein, or very, very little, and one thing leads to another—you get hired for what you're known for.

CZ: Do you have a sense of an arc in your performance style from your early performances to the present?

JL: I don't really watch myself that much. *Twilight Zone* was on TV the other day and I watched it through, and that's an unusual experience. I think it's one of my best movie performances, but I hadn't seen it in years.

CZ: It's like a complete little film.

JL: Yeah, a little short story. Very, very high powered. George Miller is a director I learned a lot from. The experience of *Twilight Zone* taught me how far I could go. It was a very liberating experience, because here was a case where at last I had a director saying, "Use everything you've got and then reach for even more." So it was the first time that I used all my theater equipment on film, and George Miller used it so brilliantly, I realized it's not always a bad thing to be big on film.

CZ: Do you find yourself interested in the technology of filmmaking? I was thinking about that as I was watching Twilight Zone, *because there are so many wild camera movements. Does that inhibit you as an actor?*

JL: No, you know what they're doing, and it tends to be very exciting. You love it when they pull off a great shot. Brian De Palma is very exciting to work with in that way. He'll spend an entire day just planning a shot and the next day shooting it.

CZ: Has De Palma been really helpful to you as an actor? You've worked with him three times, in Obsession *(1976),* Blow Out *(1981), and* Raising Cain *(1992).*

JL: Brian is an old friend; he was the one that recommended me to the director of my very first movie, *Dealing.* He saw me in a theater workshop in the summer of 1966; I was doing a Molière one-act farce, and I remember him sitting in the audience squealing with laughter. That was our first experience of each other. You talk about an arc: I've worked with him on an average of once every eight years. He's real fun to work with.

CZ: In Raising Cain, *you're playing five roles. It's like a mini-repertory. Did De Palma write it for you?*

JL: Yeah, I believe he did. Certainly he called me the minute it was a go project: "I've got your role." Brian is the maker of all sorts of brilliantly imperfect films. I enjoy the work with him very much; he really does bring me into the process.

CZ: How does he do that?

JL: Well, in *Raising Cain,* we rehearsed for a week. Not since *Garp* had I rehearsed so much for a movie. Loads and loads of things were thrown in and left out, we rewrote moments of the script, I was full of suggestions. It was my idea to make the dad a Norweigan; it was my idea to incorporate the little nursery rhyme. I had a lot of ideas that he just rejected out of hand, too, but it was an atmosphere where anything goes.

CZ: How did you get into doing mega-action films like Cliffhanger *(1993) and* Ricochet *(1991)? You really raise the level of those films!*

JL: Well, thank you. It was sort of a conscious decision between myself and my agent to try and upgrade my commercial status. You know, look what *Lethal Weapon* (1987) did for Danny Glover, or *In the Line of Fire* (1993) did for John Malkovich, or Tommy Lee Jones in *The Fugitive* (1993). Those are all top pieces; all of them are a little classier than *Ricochet*, in various ways. *Cliffhanger* certainly outgrossed them all, except *The Fugitive*. It was purely a matter of making a strategic commercial movie. I was very uneasy about it in both cases, really.

CZ: Because of the nature of the roles?

JL: Because of the nature of the movie, and the writing. In neither case was it deathless prose. You hurl yourself into it, and you think, "Well, do it for what it is. This is a big, over-the-top action adventure." They were both fun jobs; *Cliffhanger* was incredible fun.

CZ: Where were you filming?

JL: In the Dolomites, and in Rome. God, it was great. But it's also a different kettle of fish being in a Stallone film. Stallone is a nice guy, he's perfectly easy to work with, but on a Stallone film, in a way, he's in one film and everybody else is in another. It's not exactly an ensemble, and that can lead to some problems. Sometimes you just feel the indignity of it; it becomes a very hierarchical experience.

CZ: Do you mean because he gets special treatment?

JL: Well, yeah. Basically, you never feel more like a supporting player than you do in a big star vehicle, and sometimes that's an indignity, you know. You begin to feel like you're lending a touch of class to what is basically a big commercial project.

CZ: Do you have any feelings about the controversy over violence in film and TV, or about censoring the content of television programs?

JL: I think it'll all shake down. I don't have many strong opinions about it; I don't think things should be censored, because who are the arbiters? I don't think there's too much violence, and I don't think there's too much censorship. I don't think there should be more violence, and I don't think there should be more censorship. I think, in a way, it's what the market allows. I don't think violent films turn society more violent.

CZ: So you don't have any compunction about performing the very violent actions you do in either one of those films?

JL: Sometimes I feel a little icky about it, but basically, I don't mind. I think they're great big, garish morality tales. Nobody writes more violent material than William Shakespeare. Read *Titus Andronicus*, where there are rapes, and a mother is made to eat meat pies made out of her two sons, and a woman's tongue is cut out and her hands are chopped off at the wrists so she won't tell on her rapists. I mean, this is Shakespeare we're talking about! There are definitely uses of violence in dramas that are spun out of the fight between good and evil.

CZ: Who are your great heroes, or people who've really influenced you as an actor?

JL: I'm sure the biggest influence by far is my father, because it's a genetic influence as well as the work. From my father comes both the good and bad habits of a sort of stock stage acting, yeoman stage acting. I would say the other big influences on me have been the best directors I've worked with. They range from Mike Nichols to Jerry Zaks . . . Oh, God, there's so many others . . . José Quintero. . . .

CZ: What did you do with him?

JL: *Anna Christie* (1977), with Liv Ullmann. Not a successful production, but, God, it was amazing to tap into that extraordinary energy flow! John Dexter, even, who was a monster but a very exhilarating man to work with in many ways, on *M. Butterfly* (1988).

CZ: What do you think is the best-written piece that you've ever been in?

JL: *Terms of Endearment*, and certain plays, of course; *M. Butterfly* on Broadway was a huge high-water mark for me.

CZ: Did you get offered the part in the film of M. Butterfly (1993), directed by David Cronenberg?

JL: No. Never even discussed.

CZ: Was that disappointing for you?

JL: Oh, of course.

CZ: What did you think of it?

JL: I never saw it, it came and went so fast. Did you see it?

CZ: Yes.

JL: I heard it was awful.

CZ: It wasn't one of Cronenberg's better efforts.

JL: I would be dishonest if I said that wasn't a little bit of a relief to me. I don't feel good for those outstanding people, but if it had been a huge success, it really would have hurt.

CZ: Are there any film actors that you held up as icons as you were growing up?

JL: Well, I would say when I was younger, my icons were the knights in England: Gielgud and Olivier and Guinness. Those three are very different, but they're the three paradigms, in a way. I became a little skeptical, first of Gielgud and then of Olivier. Their British technique overwhelmed me after a while. I used to think they were completely magic. I will always revere Guinness; he's a wonderful combination of a great character actor and a master of restraint. You think of the extravagance of some of his early performances: Gulle Jimson in *Horse's Mouth* (1958), and Fagin in *Oliver Twist* (1948), and *Tunes of Glory* (1960), and *Bridge on the River Kwai* (1957). That's the career that I wish I had! I do in a sense, but he did so many fine, fine films. The one disappointment is that I haven't been in enough really good films.

CZ: What do you think is the biggest challenge of film acting?

JL: The biggest challenge is making bad material good, elevating bad writing. So much comes from the writing, and the hardest acting is in the worst material. If the material is good, you could be hanging upside down underwater and struggling with an octopus, and if it's well written, you're having a wonderful time!

Career Highlights

Film: *Obsession* 76. *Blow Out* 81. *The World According to Garp* (AAN) 82. *Terms of Endearment* (AAN) 83. *Twilight Zone: The Movie* 83. *The Adventures of Buckaroo Banzai* 84. *Harry and the Hendersons* 87. *At Play in the Fields of the Lord* 91. *Raising Cain* 92. *Cliffhanger* 93. *Orange County* 2001. *Shrek* 2001 (voice). *Portofino* 2002.

Theater: *The Changing Room* (Tony, Drama Desk Award) 73. *The Comedians* 76. *Anna Christie* 77. *Once in a Lifetime* 78. *Division Street* 80. *Beyond Therapy* 82. *Requiem for a Heavyweight* (Drama Desk Award) 84. *M. Butterfly* 88. *Who's Afraid of Virginia Woolf* (L.A. Critic's Award) 90.

Television: *The Day After* 83. *The Glitter Dome* 84. *World War II: When Lion's Roared* 94. *My Brother's Keeper* 95. *Don Quixote* 2000. Series: "Amazing Stories," episode (Emmy) 89. "Third Rock from the Sun" (three Emmy Awards; two SAGs; GG; American Comedy Award) 96–2001.

Mary Steenburgen

Is the work wonderful? Is the actual act of taking words and making them live and breathe a privilege? Yes. Is that so fun you can hardly bear it sometimes? Yes. Is that something you'd like to do forever? Yes. . . . I'm in it because I love it, and . . . because I really want to have a great time in this life.

CAROLE ZUCKER: *You studied at The Neighborhood Playhouse. Can you talk about that?*

MARY STEENBURGEN: Well, I went there in 1972 and I studied for two years. We got to study with Sandy Meisner maybe once or twice a week, and then in the second year you studied with him more frequently. We had acting classes every day; we had ballet, and certain modern dances inspired by Martha Graham. We studied voice and I lost a great deal of my southern accent, which was very, very thick when I came, and which I knew would limit me as an actress.

The training begins as a series of improvisational exercises that Sandy Meisner devised. And the goal of the exercises is to cause people to really begin to act, without doing all the things that people innately start doing when they hear the word *act*, which usually involves posing, and self-consciousness, and trying to be good. Sandy's exercises call you back to an instinct that you have as a child, before you become encumbered with self-consciousness and a judgmental attitude about yourself and others. When a kid is playing cowboys, and they go "bang-bang," they just drop dead. They don't say, "Gee, what kind of gun is that?" or "I'm not sure I believe that," or "You weren't pointing it directly at me," they just drop dead; they play. I think that we lose a great deal of this, and we become much more self-conscious and inward-looking as we grow older. With most people, the initial approach to acting immediately turns you in on your self; you look inward. Sandy's exercises, which are very simple and very uncomplicated, and very—well, excuse me, but—free of bullshit, are designed to cause you to tell the truth under imaginary circumstances, and to focus on the person that you're with, as opposed to yourself. Most actors trained by Sandy Meisner are really affected by the other actors in the piece with them, in a way that is completely spontaneous.

One of the things I loved about Sandy, as opposed to other acting teachers—who I think mess with people's heads too much, and potentially kill off really wonderful instincts—is that his training was designed to be a support for all your great instincts. And he loves it if you bring new ideas, or throw things out, and make additions or subtractions from what he's giving you. It's never failed me as a basis for my work, as a place to start from.

CZ: What were your ambitions when you went to The Neighborhood Playhouse?

MS: I lied about my earliest ambition when I went there. I told people at home I was going to study to be a teacher. The reason I said that was it was too big a dream; it almost sounded like a little girl's fantasy to say, "I'm going to be an actress," coming from somebody who'd never met an actress in her life. You have to realize that for me, they were mythical creatures, they weren't people who really earned a living that way. I justified my trip to New York by saying that I was going to go learn to be a great theater teacher, and the truth was I always wanted to be an actress.

CZ: Were your parents supportive of your decision to act?

MS: I just am one of those lucky people that got dream parents. My father was a freight train conductor, and an incredible man. My mother is still alive. She's a wonderful pal, a sweet woman. When I said I wanted to go be an actress, they were totally supportive—"Wow, we can't wait to see what you're going to do." I've tested a lot over the years; I've done a lot of things that maybe some people would have found embarrassing, and also thrown the good and bad parts of being famous into their laps. They've had to deal with all that, and they've been incredible. When I went to The Neighborhood Playhouse, I think I was one of the only kids that went there with total approval, as opposed to parents who said, "Go try this for a couple of years, and then we'll see what happens."

CZ: *Did you have any aspirations to go into film when you were at* The Neighborhood Playhouse?

MS: No more than most young girls do. I had those nights where I had felt belittled by somebody, or I hated the way I looked, or whatever, and I would have fantasies about how "I'll just grow up to be a movie star, and I'll show them." But I don't think there's a little girl or boy who doesn't say that, who dreams about being something that's going to show some-body else. The irony was, when it actually did happen, I didn't feel vin-dictive towards anybody! I haven't felt like I showed anybody anything! My struggles are still my struggles, and being a so-called movie star doesn't make your pain any less, or anything else; it's still a real life. So, in that sense, it wasn't what I might have thought it was going to be.

Being at The Playhouse was an amazing time for me, first of all, be-cause I had gone from Arkansas to "the Great City of New York" and I was going to standing-room-only seats in theaters and seeing amazing performances of actors, and off-off-Broadway theaters, and all kinds of experimental plays. I was really driven and excited, just wildly obsessed with theater. I didn't study or know anything about film at that point; I didn't ever dream that's what I would end up doing.

CZ: *What was it was like to work on your first film,* Goin' South *(1978)?*

MS: Well, it's funny, because there are no words big enough to describe that time in my life. By the time this happened, I had been in New York around six years, studying and working and waitressing. And it was as though I said, "I want to fly to the moon," and I had been saying that every single day for many years. And then suddenly one night, some-one came and tapped me on my shoulder, and before I could put my bathrobe on or grab my toothbrush, they said, "This is the time your dreams come true; you get to fly to the moon." And, yes, I'd always wanted to fly to the moon, but I needed to get my life in order, or say goodbye to somebody, or prepare for what it's going to be like with no gravity. When it came, it came like *that* [snaps fingers]. I don't mean stardom came so much, because *Goin' South* was not a terribly success-ful movie. But I was the female lead in the movie opposite a huge movie star, and I had never been around a movie star. And I had never been on a film set; and I had never been in front of a film camera; and I didn't know what all the names of the jobs were; and I didn't know what "hit your marks" meant. When I'd got a little house in Durango, where we were shooting, I didn't know how to have a maid. I didn't know how to deal with my mother when she called me up at four o'clock in the morning because she'd read in the newspaper that Jack Nicholson and I had run off and gotten married. I didn't know anything. All I had was this incredible training, and an amazing twenty-four-year history of love and support, which was a lot.

Every single thing I dealt with was new. And the technical things weren't as hard as the emotional things. You know, learning how to hit your marks, even though you can't look down at them, which is one of the great incongruities of film. That was easy compared to learning where I belonged in the world now. Who are my friends? Who's jealous of me, and who isn't? Who is going to say, the first time I'm late returning a phone call, "Well, she's gone Hollywood now." All that was much harder to learn. It took years, actually.

And Jack was an incredible teacher; and I'm lucky that if I was going to be so-called discovered by somebody, it was somebody who was so immensely gifted himself. He was very generous, he didn't try to hoard his secrets and his experience to himself, he just gave it generously to me. Jack screened films at Paramount for me, and he would come in and ask me questions about them, "Why was that great, why did that actress do that, what did she do there with her eyes that she could have done a different way?" He gave me an incredible film acting workshop in those months before we started shooting. After we watched films, Jack took me over to the screening room and showed me my dailies, and taught me something about editing and how to use the camera better. So that now, I hope most editors will tell you that I'm conscious of giving them cuts when I work. I'll turn my head in a certain way, or do something at the end of the take so they have a place to cut.

This time for me was agony and ecstasy. I was doing all I could do to stay above water. And I really wanted to be good, and to live up to Jack's belief in me. He had been the first person that really validated what I felt I had inside. And so it was intensely important to me not to disappoint him.

CZ: What do you see now when you watch Goin' South?

MS: Now, I can barely watch the film, because I see me, Mary, being so incredibly vulnerable that I almost can't watch it without cringing. [laughs] I think that everybody has in them a first really pure performance. That doesn't mean that after that you're just a big sham, but I think that the first time you do a performance like that, it's like the first time you make love. You're a virgin one time, and I was a virgin in film one time, and that was *Goin' South*. I can look at that film and see everything about my life in it. I can see how I felt about Jack, that I hero-worshipped him, I can see my excitement, and my pride, and my terror, and my incredible vulnerability. And to me, they're all somehow woven into that performance.

CZ: I often find Jack Nicholson's acting very heightened, and that's certainly true in Goin' South. *Did you feel that you were being asked to adjust your performance because of that?*

MS: I think that I will always adjust to another actor's style, because I'm hopefully always connected to that actor. It's the way I work; I never determine something before a film and just go in there, and come hell or high water, do it. I try to know who the character is; I try to know things about her. What sort of person she is, what she would like, what her background is, and how she feels about life. I trust in all that when I stand in front of the other person, and the camera. But I trust that all that work has been done, and I don't act upon that. I act upon what I'm given from the other person. I have something called "actor's faith," which is that all the preliminary work has been done and is in there. So I'm never thinking about motivation, or family history, or any of that stuff, when I'm working. I'm thinking about "Why is he looking at me like that? Why is his eyebrow standing up? Is he lying to me?" Whatever it is that I'm going through with that character, with that other actor, that's what my mind's on, not style, or background, or anything else. Because of that, I think that I cannot help but be affected by the style of anybody who works around me. I'm sure it's probably true that I might be more heightened if somebody else is.

CZ: Are you saying that you've already internalized the ideas about the character before you shoot?

MS: I put it in the same way you put it into a computer, and then I just trust that it's there. I don't act from notes. If you look at my scripts, there are no suggestions written to myself about what to do at any moment. Because I don't know what I'm going to do. There may be notes about "it's 'as if' so and so." I use *as if* a lot, which is something Sandy uses. It's a way of personalizing something, "It's as if it's Lily's [Mary's daughter] tenth birthday and I don't get to make it there," or something like that. If I think of an idea that will help me to personalize something, I might make a note about that. But I won't say, "And that makes me stomp around the room" or "That makes me cry." I don't ever know what I'm going to do, and so far, I've been lucky enough to work with directors who have respected that, who wait, and say, "Well, let's see what happens." It would be real hard for me to work with somebody that just talked in result terms, because I don't know what the results are going to be.

CZ: How do you choose projects? Do you have any overall plan in terms of your career goals?

MS: To be really honest with you—and this doesn't sound very artistic, or it sounds like I'm maybe less of an artist than I would like to think I am—now I figure in things like when my children are out of school, and if somebody's offering me something to do on the kids' spring break. I mean, I'm a mother, and it's really important to me. And I'm really aware that I have one childhood for each of these kids. The person that I described to you, that went to New York and was so obsessed with learning her craft, I am not that person any more. Do I still care intensely about my work, and do I have a lot of integrity about it? I hope anybody that's worked with me will tell you that I do. But do I think that the most important thing in the world now is acting? No. It is certainly, besides my children, my greatest joy. I have never been bored for one second on a film set. I love it, but I also recognize that I gave birth to two children and I want their lives to be great, and it can't be great if I'm working all the time. So I've really chosen to limit my career.

I don't want to turn around at seventy years old and realize I have these important credits. I want to look back and say, "Boy, I had a good, fun life." I've always held that very close, and never let go of it.

CZ: But what attracts you to one script and not another?

MS: There's one truth that's always remained the same, as far as how I choose scripts, and that is, I try to do things that make my heart beat a little faster. When I read them, there's something about it that's fun, or engaging, or I wanted to work with a certain director, or because I found an element in the script challenging or difficult.

CZ: How did you get involved in Melvin and Howard *(1980)? That has a wonderful script.*

MS: That screenplay, which won Bo Goldman the Best Screenplay Academy Award, is still the best screenplay I've ever read. Jack Nicholson gave it to me as an example of great writing. Nobody sent it to me. I read it, and I was determined to play that part. I went in and I read for Jonathan Demme, and I got it because I did this really great reading. Including at the end of the reading, grabbing Paul Le Mat's [Melvin's] face, and pulling his face down to mine, and giving him the biggest kiss he's ever had in his life, and walking out of the room. By the time I got home, Jonathan called me and said, "There's no point making you wait; I want you to play that part."

CZ: How do you approach your characters, and specifically, how did you prepare for the role of Linda in Melvin and Howard?

MS: The first time I read a script is really an important moment for me, and I actually treat it in a little bit of a precious way. I don't read scripts and watch TV at the same time. In fact, I don't do anything when I read a script except read the script. Not only because I'm respectful of writers, but also because I find that it's the most pure time for me in terms of my approach to the material. Because I don't know what's around the corner. In films, or theater, or literature, once you've read something, you know what's going to happen. And actually I'm in a process of trying to forget that I know what's around the corner, because in life we don't. The first time I read something I find I really listen to all my instincts, and all my first responses. Because, even though, in retrospect, they may seem naïve, they were true for that moment, with that lack of knowledge about how everything turns out in the end.

All kinds of things happened to me the first time I read *Melvin and Howard,* including falling in love with Linda. I find that I love all my characters, including the ones that nobody else loves, like the one in *Miss Firecracker* (1989), who was despicable. [laughter] When I did *Tender Is the Night* [a BBC television production], everybody kept calling me crazy, and I would look at them like they were crazy, because I didn't see Nicole Diver as crazy. Once I saw her as crazy, I would have been distancing myself from her. I understood why she did everything that she did. What I always do is approach things symphonically; I will figure it out like a

piece of music, in the same way you'd take a piece of sheet music and figure out where's the crescendo, decrescendo, pianissimo. Because you can't
do it scene by scene. If you do it scene by scene, it's not seamless when
it's put together. If you just act your little heart out in every scene, it won't
work. A script has to have highs and lows. There are scenes that aren't my
scenes, they're somebody else's scenes, and there are scenes that "Boy, I
better get in there and really make a strong moment." You can only do
that by starting with the whole piece, and working it out, so that when it
gets broken up and split apart—because we rarely do anything in chro-
nological order—you always know where you are.

I also like to work physically, to give myself a physical task for a character if I can. When I did *Melvin and Howard*, I tap-danced and tried to
get really good enough to control how bad I was. I hoped that the end
product would be fun; not a truly brilliant tap-dancer, but somebody
who's really putting her heart and soul into it. But in order to control
that, I had to be better than that, so I really worked hard at tap-dancing,
every single day for a month.

*CZ: The way that you're working with objects is so real-looking. I was
thinking of the scene where you make a hero sandwich for your daughter in
about thirty seconds.*

MS: It was so real I cut my finger in the scene! [laughter] If you really look
closely, you can see that it's not all ketchup on the bread.

CZ: Would that be something that you would practice?

MS: I don't know how much I practiced, but I know that there's a way of
doing everything. Linda is a completely earthbound, organic person, who
has had to make lots of sandwiches and stuff; she knows how to do that,
even though she'd rather be dancing. Whatever you do tells the truth
about her, in the same way that when I made a cup of tea before, you
could either tell I've made a lot of cups of tea or I haven't. The same is
true of these people, because every action speaks of all their life, not just
their two-hour life that you get a chance to see.

Actually, if you asked me at the time, how did I approach the character, I would have told you, I remember saying that it was very simple, that
the character loved to dance. I try to boil things down to their simplest
and their strongest forms. I don't like to act "Well, it's sorta this, and it's
sorta that." I like to have things very distilled and very powerful in my

mind when I work. As an actress I don't like to feel confused, I like to feel very clear. Sometimes my characters may be confused, but as far as how I'm approaching them, I like clarity.

I like the idea, "Why is this day different than any other day?" I'm not crazy about naturalistic acting that's about "a day in the life of." I think that you go to films to be taken away. Sometimes that's by enlightenment, and sometimes that's just by laughing your head off at something that's ridiculous and silly. If it effectively transports you, then the actors and directors have done their own little magic. I don't like doing things in a casual, naturalistic way. I remember saying in that sandwich scene, "When you get there tell Nell and Morris. . . ." That's my parents. I play around with stuff like that, without managing to come out of a scene. I'm aware that I have the privilege of being able to say hello to my unborn descendants. I get to say "hi" to my childrens' childrens' childrens' children. I have little moments where I'm aware that if film exists, and survives, and if any of my films do, that people who are somehow friendly will watch them. I love thinking about things like that when I work. I love all the different layers you can play with. But that scene was nice.

Actually, my favorite moment, I think, in my film career so far, is in that movie. And I know that Bo Goldman feels the same way, as far as a line reading of his work. It's the scene where I say, "Well, c'est la vie, Melvin." I so love that piece of writing, and I really tried to rise to that moment. I think I could never repeat it. Melvin says, "Well, what's that mean?" and I say, "It's French. I used to dream of being a French interpreter." "You don't speak French," and I say, "I told you, it was a dream." That moment just came out of something that's so deep in me, and also deep in Bo Goldman. It says a lot about who I was and who I am, and it came without any obstruction, and I am very proud of it.

CZ: Did Jonathan Demme talk to you about the tone of your performance? In one scene, you're sitting, drinking a brandy in the middle of the afternoon, watching a game show on TV. Melvin asks you what's for dinner, you say, "Bell peppers," and he says, "You know I don't like bell peppers." What's there is a conflict and antagonism, but it's done in a very understated way.

MS: Sometimes, the words may come out in a very simple way, but what's behind them isn't simple. We may be talking about bell peppers, but we're talking about our lives, and our frustrations, and the marriage, and my big dreams, and how they're not coming true. I don't remember so much that Jonathan—and this is true of most of the directors I've worked with, the good ones—told me how to do anything, so much as gave me an amazing arena in which to do it. The arena is amazing because they choose great production people. You walk into a house and you say, "This is exactly what Linda's house would look like," or, you can make some small suggestions and they're open and they hear you.

And Jonathan made me feel safe. If the director doesn't make you feel safe—and to a certain degree, actors are a little bit like children, and we're asked to play like children —if they don't give you a place that feels supportive of that, where you won't be ridiculed, where you're not worried that they're judging you; if they don't give you that, you can't fly. So I don't think it's so much what they say to you, it's what they give you, it's where they give you to play. It's not really words so much as support, and their artistic choices so far as your backdrop, the painting that you're in. Jonathan's a master at that. There's something to look at in every single shot, some crazy little whimsical funny thing that's got his stamp on it. He and Bo were brilliant at providing me with things to do.

I am at my best, and I think all actors are, when you're given something great to do. "The seed of the craft of acting is the reality of doing." That's the first thing Sandy Meisner said to me. And it's the truth. And so when you were asking me about that scene in the bus depot, I really did make about twenty sandwiches, I wasn't just pretending. When I was tap-dancing as though I had gone on a game show, everything about that felt real to me. Partly, you have to give Jonathan credit for things like casting Bob Ridgely, who was brilliant as the game show host, he couldn't have been better. He made that real for me, and I worked off of him, and I used him, and I took what he gave me. Most of that was improvisational, all the interviewing, all the "Where are you from?" "Would you like to put your hands in Uncle Wally's pocket?" All that was just playing together.

CZ: Do you ever make a distinction in your own mind between art and entertainment? Let's take a film like Back to the Future Part III *(1990).*

MS: Yes, that's entertainment. But within that, the people I was working with worked as hard as a lot of people that are so-called artists. They didn't phone it in at all; they really thought about it. They made the film essentially for nine-year-old boys; that's their target audience. And they really think about what nine-year-old boys like, and address that. And nothing was cheap. My costumes were totally researched, and the color of the purple in the train was a color that had been introduced from Paris that very year. The quality of the people that worked on that film was as good as anything I've ever done. It didn't feel like I was just doing this commercial movie where nobody really cared. They cared very much.

I think that, essentially, when we get too highbrow about what we're there to do, we've lost something. If you talk to someone like Lauren Bacall, she doesn't want to talk to you about artists. She wants to talk about "Was it funny, was it good, did people enjoy it?" I respect the down-to-earthness of the people that were ahead of me, and the way that they didn't get too pretentious about what they do. There's this little framed print that's in my bedroom, and it says, "Angels fly because they take themselves lightly." The reason it's there is because I tend not to like people that take themselves too seriously, especially in this business. There's a balance between recognizing that what you do should be entertaining, and yes, sometimes thought-provoking, and maybe challenging, and also trying to do it as well as you can. So that if I do *Back to the Future*, I try to make every moment as true as I can.

Listen, I'm in it because I love it, and I'm also in it because I really want to have a great time in this life. And everybody that's ever worked with me will tell you that it's really important to me to have fun on a film. And it shows in the movie. It's three months of my life! This thing about suffering for your art, if I ever did think it was true, then I suppose it may have been true for the first, early years of my life, but now I don't believe in it. To me, it's a joyous enterprise. And I'm lucky as hell to get to do it.

CZ: How do you deal with the fame involved in being a film actor?

MS: I realized even before I had children that being famous or being a successful actor was not what people thought it was. Is the work wonderful? Is the actual act of taking words and making them live and breathe a privilege? Yes. Is that so fun you can hardly bear it sometimes? Yes. Is that something you'd like to do forever? Yes. Somebody coming up and asking you for your autograph, does that make you feel better about yourself? No. Does that mean when you're having a bad day, you're feeling sad or lonely, does the recognition make you feel better? No. Does reading an article or an interview about yourself, or seeing your name all over the papers, does that make you feel more important, more significant? No, it doesn't.

So the whole thing that people go into it for, for me, I quickly saw, was a myth. It didn't exist. It didn't do one thing for me. I saw that the only thing left that was truthful about it was the work itself. That the work itself just tickled me to death, and it was an incredible mental and emotional and personal challenge. That got better, but all that other stuff doesn't amount to very much. And I feel like I've lived fully. I think it's very easy, in this business, to surrender your life to a career, and I won't do it.

CZ: Do you ever study performances by the actors who went before you?

MS: That's part of my ongoing education. There is so much to be learned by watching some of the great film performances of this century, as much as anything anybody can tell you in a book, or anything you can see today. I've never not gotten something from watching the great actors work, never. Somebody on film like Spencer Tracy, or Jimmy Stewart, or Jean Arthur, or Montgomery Clift, or any of the great people whose performances are preserved—to not take advantage of that is to say, "Well, I'm going to limit what I do." And I would never do that. I'll listen to anybody who's going to offer a suggestion or give me an idea that I can use in my work. It doesn't mean I'll use it, but I would never cut off a supply line of something that can make me a better actress. I just feel like I've put a toe in the water. I'd be very sad if this is as good as I'm going to get.

Career Highlights

Film: *Goin' South* 78. *Time After Time* 79. *Melvin and Howard* (AA) 80. *Ragtime* 81. *A Midsummer Night's Sex Comedy* 82. *Cross Creek* 83. *Miss Firecracker* 89. *Parenthood* 89. *Back to the Future: Part III* 90. *What's Eating Gilbert Grape* 93. *Pontiac Moon* 94. *The Grass Harp* 95. *Nixon* 95. *Absolute Zero* 2000. *Wish You Were Dead* 2000. *Life As a House* 2001. *Nobody's Baby* 2001. *Sunshine State* 2001.

Theater: *Candida* 93. *Marvin's Room* 94. *The Beginning of August* 2000.

Television: *Tender Is the Night* (British Broadcaster's Guild Award) 85. *The Attic: The Hiding of Anne Frank* 88. *Gulliver's Travels* 96. *About Sarah* (SAGN) 98. *Picnic* 2000.

Tom Conti

*A performance has got to be done with the same concentra-
tion as a driver of a Formula One racing car. That's how
hard you have to think.*

CAROLE ZUCKER: *What was the cultural climate like when you were
growing up? You were a child during the war years and after, really.*

TOM CONTI: I grew up in Glasgow, went to school there, a private Catholic
boys' school. Yuck. Actually, there wasn't anything particularly wrong with
this school. I think it was probably the only civilized Catholic boys' school
there. It's difficult for me to know what the cultural life was like generally in
Glasgow. For me, it was very good, because my parents were fairly cultured
people. Theater, music, opera, and concerts were all part of my upbringing,
my childhood, which is why I do what I do, I suppose.

CZ: *So it's your parents who influenced you most to become an actor?*

TC: I think it's everybody's parents who influence them, deeply. It's what you
offer the empty brain, really, that is important, and that will continue to grow
in later life.

CZ: *Were there any teachers that particularly encouraged you? Did you do any
acting in secondary school?*

TC: Yes. That's where the bug bit, I suppose. I had a maths master who loved
opera, and occasionally we would see each other at concerts, which was interesting, because at school we could talk about something other than logarithm tables,
and so I liked him for that. He was quite a cultured guy.

There were other teachers who were interesting. I actually got a letter five years ago from an English teacher who had just decided to write after all these years. She had a wonderful name, Miss Weeple. She said she remembered that when I read Shakespeare in class I somehow made sense of it. One of the nice things about being an actor, that suddenly letters will pop out of the blue. And I'm not attached to Shakespeare.

CZ: Let's hold that thought for later, because I know you have strong opinions about the subject. You went to the Royal Scottish Academy in Glasgow. Was that a conscious decision; did you want to remain in Scotland?

TC: It never occurred to me to do anything else. In fact, I went to join the Royal Scottish Academy in music, and somehow drifted into the Drama department.

CZ: What kind of music were you interested in?

TC: Classical music. That's what I'd always wanted to do, what I always thought I would do. But life takes funny turns, and it's probably a great mercy for the world of music that I became an actor.

CZ: What sort of place was the Royal Scottish Academy? What was their orientation?

TC: I think what set it apart from a lot of other drama schools—obviously I didn't go to them, but I've talked to people who did—was that the accent was on practicality. Maybe that has something to do with the Scottish nature of the place. If you were lucky enough to have a talent, then that was fine. It was there or not. If it was there, then they tried to teach you to use it effectively. It seemed to me to make very good sense. If you're going to be a painter and you don't know how to mix the paint, it's going to take you an awfully long time to get anywhere. The same with fiddle-playing—you've got to master the technique, otherwise, no music. It's the same with an actor. If your technique is not well honed, then it's never going to work. You'll have to stumble your way through.

There was one particular tutor there that I liked very much, although he was also completely terrifying. He taught you to analyze the things that need to be analyzed. Practical things like, after the performance: "Why didn't you get a laugh on that line?" I'd say, "I don't know," and he'd say, "Well, think about it." Then he'd say, "What did you do? Did you say the line and then turn away or did you turn away and then say the line?" So, "I think I turned away and then said the line," and he'd say, "Well yes, that's why you didn't get the laugh." A lot of it is natural anyway, but sometimes you do make mistakes, and you have to know what to do.

CZ: It's very technical.

TC: It's vital. Don't let anybody kid you that acting isn't technical. It is. If it's not, it's a mess. There are schools and various methods, but they're all technical. The most technical man in the world was Lee Strasberg. I mean, if *that* wasn't technical, tell me what is.

CZ: I'm not sure I understand what you mean when you use the word technical, *if you think Lee Strasberg was technical.*

TC: It was a technique. The part of acting that makes it interesting is the complicated part you can't teach. That's what makes De Niro or Hackman, or people of that ilk, great actors, and eminently watchable. There's a bit that they know that most actors don't know. You can't teach that bit. You can teach a lot of the other stuff; and these methods are really for the guys who can't do it. And it helps them to do it a bit. But Marlon Brando would have been Marlon Brando if he'd gone to a Scottish Country Dance Academy instead of Lee Strasberg. Exactly the same thing would have come out, because the man is immensely talented.

I'm very much against all that stuff . . . method. I mean acting is a very simple thing. It's pretending to be . . . whatever . . . a fireman. So, let's pretend the tree is a house, and I'll be a fireman and come up and rescue you, and get to see your knickers at the same time. Acting is the same thing, except that they actually go and get a house, set it on fire, give you a fire engine, and a uniform and you do exactly the same thing. But for the same game it has cost for that day—$140,000. [laughs] It's just an extension of "let's pretend." We're all nuts, really.

CZ: There still seems to be the controversy about British acting versus American acting, that the British act from the head, and the Americans from the guts.

TC: Good actors just act, with everything there is. Most actors can't do it. It's the same in acting as it is in tennis or piano playing. Look at the population of the world, and then look at how many really, really great pianists there are—a handful. Though there are lots of terribly good ones, the rest muddle along as best they can.

CZ: So you don't think that there's any quintessence of British acting?

TC: Yes. A lot of it is extremely boring. As lots of American acting is extremely boring. The trouble with actors is that they act. The skill is *not* to show the acting. But there's a great temptation, because they feel they ought to be doing *something;* they're paid for it, so they've got to show *something.* So they act.

The great problem with the Brits as movie actors is English Classical acting. I would stamp it out tomorrow. It's just a passport to nowhere, and it makes them unable to perform properly, because they're so busy performing, and so busy portraying, that they miss the essential point about acting, which is to provoke the imagination of the watcher in such a way that the watcher will do your work for you. Simply that.

CZ: When you say actors are "performing," what precisely does that mean to you?

TC: I find British Classical acting tiresome. I just don't believe it, and it doesn't involve me emotionally. I don't think it involves the audience emotionally, generally. When you do Shakespeare, you're forgiven almost everything. People suspend their normal critical faculties when watching Shakespeare. They accept degrees of unreality that would normally cause them to leave at the first intermission. They let the actors get away with extravagant nonsense, then go out of the theater saying, "Oh, it was a great performance." Of course, I don't deny that acting Shakespeare has its problems. We don't go around speaking in iambic pentameter, for instance, and we are, in most cases, able to tell boys from girls, unlike many of Shakespeare's characters who seem a lamentably unobservant bunch.

The *in-depth* thing for the most part happens naturally with actors. The understanding of a script, or what the Royal Shakespeare Company call "the text," is simple. Mostly, it means what it says. I once watched a Shakespeare acting workshop on television—a couple of actors being directed by a Shakespeare expert. When the actors started to read for the first time, they made a fair stab at it; it was believable and understandable. Then the "expert" started on them, and in no time at all destroyed any truth that the actors originally had. Well, that's wrong.

CZ: But how can you hope to do that job unless you understand what the text is about?

TC: But you do; it's easy to understand what the text is about. There are parts in every play which are wholly incomprehensible, and a blue pencil should go through them immediately. It should all be chucked out so that the play makes sense to everybody.

During rehearsal for *The Beaux Strategem* by Farquhar, there was a scene which was just impossible, impossible because none of us knew what it meant. We kept rehearsing and eventually I said to the director, "We should cut the scene. If you tell me what it means, and particularly what *that* speech means, and what it's there for, then I'll do it. Otherwise, I'm not going to do it, right?" and, of course, he couldn't. So that was the end of it. People soldier on because they are dealing with a classic, and it was written a long time ago. It's like religion. Because it was written a long time ago, they accept it. They believe Mary was a virgin because it happened two thousand years ago. If someone told you it happened last Wednesday, you'd say, "Don't be bloody stupid!"

CZ: Do you think there's any merit in people going to see Shakespeare?

TC: Yes! Listen, the best Shakespeare I ever saw was Meryl Streep and Kevin Kline. They were stunning.

CZ: In The Taming of the Shrew?

TC: Yes, they didn't torture it to death. Jimmy Cagney was wonderful as Bottom in *A Midsummer's Night Dream* (1935), all those years ago. He was interviewed on British television, and it was terrific. They said, "What preparation did you make?" He said, "Well, I learned it. . . ." And they said, "But what preparation did you make?" He said, "What do you mean?" They said, "Well, this is Shakespeare," and he said, "This is just another script." That's what it should be—just another script.

CZ: So you're of the school that says: "Put both feet on the floor, say the lines, and don't bump into the furniture"?

TC: It's not nearly as simple as that. When you read a book—if it's a properly written book—you see everything. The man says, "I was walking down the street, it was raining. . . ." You're *there*. You see "the man," you see "the street," you see "the rain." You feel the atmosphere. That is what we actors are supposed to do—give you a sketch and not interfere with your imagination. If I'm receiving the news that my entire village has been wiped out by the plague, my family dead, and an actor attempts to portray a large emotion, then he's blown it. He has interfered with the audience's own vision of the horror. The imagination of members of the audience is, for the most part, far superior to the actor's ability to "portray."

CZ: What is it that bothers you about "the method"?

TC: It's too complicated. I cannot tell you the contortions that actors go through in their minds to get something out. This is supposed to be *easy*. It's supposed to be good fun. You're not supposed to torture yourself and have a bad time; and so many youngsters do. They imagine that there is information which we all have to which they are not privy, and sadly, a great many acting teachers support them in that error. Acting is at once highly complicated and extremely simple. The simple bit you can teach people. The complicated bit, no amount of tuition will ever elucidate. If it ain't in you, it ain't in you.

The idea of employing "sense memory" is to me an unnecessary confusion. Just listen to what the other actor is saying and respond accordingly. Do what you think a human being would do in whatever the situation is. That's basically all it is.

CZ: Do you feel that you work a lot off the other actor?

TC: There's nothing else *to* work off. Nothing. Sometimes you have to make it up if the other actor is not delivering.

CZ: When you work on pieces where there is virtually no backstory—for example, in Pinter's The Dumbwaiter *(1987), which you made with Robert Altman—do you make up something to help yourself along?*

TC: You don't even have to make it up. It just chunks into your head. You don't have to think, "Where did he come from?" When you read it, you know. When I read Gus, I knew what he was. I made up what he was like *that* [snaps fingers] as I read it. There was no other searching. I didn't sit down and make a list of what his life was like, not at all. You either see the man or you don't. I saw this little guy who had designed this little life for himself. He combed his hair and tried to be neat and tidy, and that's his world. That's what I saw when I read it.

CZ: Do you think Pinter is unusual in how little backstory he supplies to the actor?

TC: Nobody gives very much.

CZ: Would you say the same is true of Neil Simon?

TC: Well, he tells you what that person does for a living. There'll occasionally be remarks about "my mom . . ." or stuff like that, but it's very sketchy. But he knows it all, and when the actor reads it, they know it all. And the audience recognizes it. They make up what they're not given. That's the great thing about the human imagination. It's good at making things up. All it needs is guidelines. And it builds the rest itself.

Harold [Pinter] hated the movie *The Dumbwaiter*, by the way. He said it was my fault. I said, "I'm sorry to hear that; why is that?" And he said, "You said seven of my lines and 125 of your own." I said, "Oh, c'mon, that's ridiculous." He said, "Do you have a copy of the play?" I say, "Yes." I counted forty-five textual inaccuracies, which, of course, in Harold's book, is a lot. There are things like "maybe" instead of "perhaps," a grunt instead of a "but." We tried to learn the lines. We sat in this very hotel, John Travolta and I, for over a week beforehand. All day, every day, battering these lines into our heads, because Pinter is very difficult to learn. And you've got to shoot this thing in two weeks. You survive. You don't stop because I say "maybe" instead of "perhaps," and say "Could we have another take please?" You just don't do that. Movies are different. If Harold was all that keen, he should've bloody well been there on the floor. No one told the script girl that Harold wanted us pulled up on any tiny inaccuracy.

CZ: Do you find that, in general, there's a lot of improvisation on films?

TC: Yes, and films are sometimes the better for it because of the way the dialogue is written. Stage writers write a different way from film writers. And with good stage writers, you don't have to touch a word. Not a single word. But a lot of the craft of great screen writing has been lost, I'm afraid. And part of that is because actors were suddenly allowed, when the studio contract system fell apart, to start changing lines. You can understand an author, a screenwriter, thinking, "I don't think I'll bother staying up till four o'clock in the morning honing this because some bloody actor's going to get hold of it in the morning and tear it to bits."

CZ: What would you say is the apogee of writing for you?

TC: In theater, I would say Simon Gray. I think he's just stunning. So is Christopher Hampton. For television, Freddie [Frederic] Raphael, although he's not really a television writer, he's a screenwriter. But the work I did for him, *Glittering Prizes* (1976), was on television. Neil Simon, again, is a complete master; the words just flow. And Harold—I think that *The Dumbwaiter* is a stupendous play. It's gloriously funny, and dense and deep, and enjoyable. If you don't do it in what they call "Pinteresque" fashion. If you do it for real. As soon as you try to do Pinter-acting; it's a disaster. It's like Shakespeare.

CZ: Do you feel you have a natural proclivity to be funny? Did you find that true since you were a child?

TC: Yes, I think so.

CZ: Do you feel you have very little inclination to explore your dark side?

TC: Very.

CZ: There are some things you've done, like Whose Life Is It Anyway? *(1978) and* Chapter Two *(1996), where there's humor combined with a very dark strain. And certainly,* Merry Christmas, Mr. Lawrence *(1983). . . .*

TC: Well, they're serious plays. Absolutely.

CZ: Have you ever yearned to get more angst-filled roles?

TC: Yes, if they were there. Actually, *Chapter Two* is filled with angst. George is an angst-ridden human being, but he has that wonderful thing—that Jewish thing—you know, laughing while hell's fire is licking at his feet, making jokes. But they all come out of pain.

The best drama is a serious subject filled with humor, wit. People like that more than anything else. That's why the likes of Christopher Hampton and Simon Gray are so hugely successful, because that's what they deliver, that's the way they see life. All of Ayckborn's characters too are filled with pain. All these people are in agony, they don't know how to live their lives; they pretend to live. They do what they think they should be doing. It's killing them, but they can't do anything about it. That's what real drama is.

CZ: Are you an actor who likes rehearsal?

TC: No. Not at all.

CZ: Why not?

TC: I just want to get to it. Also, I can't stand discussions at rehearsal. I just can't bear it. Get on with it, say it, learn it, speak it. It'll come to you if you just keep doing it. But if we sit and talk about it for two hours, you'll get more distant from it. You'll only get confused. And that applies to all texts.

CZ: Do you think the same laws apply to film and the theater?

TC: Film is very different. The reason we have a three or four week rehearsal period in the theater, or six or seven weeks in the case of the National Theatre, three of which are a complete waste of time, is because you have to learn a whole play. And the easiest way to learn it is by doing it over and over again. Good, well-written stuff goes into your head very easily. Curious how Shakespeare is very easy to learn. It's because, again, the man was a very good writer.

And people like Hampton write dialogue that is very easy to learn. You do a scene, you practically know it by the time you've got to the end of it. You don't have to sit at home pounding it into your head. Still, if it's two hours long, you have two hours of dialogue to learn. It's quite a chunk, so you rehearse. Also, the whole play has to have a cohesion to it, a shape. But in film, you do it in bits; you learn the scene the night before or in the car on the way to location. You might only have five words in a whole day. "Oh my god, there's something on the . . . ." And then the train plunges over the ravine. And it takes a whole week to film the train.

CZ: Yes, but you've also been in films like Reuben, Reuben *(1982), where there's been a lot of dialogue.*

TC: Yes, it was a lot of dialogue, but even if you rehearsed for a week before shooting, when you're finally on the set, a completely different motor is switched on in everybody's brain. It's called "the performance engine," if you like. "Click, vroom," this thing starts, and everything you did at rehearsal goes out the window, because suddenly you're doing it. There's an immediacy, a tension, and the scene is completely different. And then you say, "Why the hell did we sit in that room for all those hours?" Sometimes what they euphemistically call "rehearsal" is in fact getting the script right, and in that respect it is useful, but it is tedious because you know you're doing it because the writing isn't good enough.

That's the wonderful thing about *Reuben;* it was written by Julius Epstein, who wrote such treasures as *Casablanca* (1942); he's just a great writer. He knows how to hone a scene. He knows how to structure a picture.

CZ: What do you think is an ideal actor–director relationship?

TC: Encouragement for each other, really. Obviously, it helps if both are intelligent people, and not swamped by ego problems and power-play ideas. People who get on, and understand the material, and help each other to achieve a goal.

CZ: Has there ever been a confrontational situation—what they call in Hollywood "creative differences" [Tom laughs]—between you and either a director or another actor? How do you deal with those situations?

TC: Well, there's Harold. It's sort of unresolvable, really. You muddle through the best you can. I think from that point of view, we Brits, certainly of my generation, were at a disadvantage, because one is brought up to do the best you can. To try to be fair and not "sink the boat." Whereas Americans were brought up in a different way, I think: to push through what they think is right and devil take the hindmost.

There were times when I should have actually had the director removed from a movie. I should have said, "Look I'm off or he's off because he's destroying the picture, so what are you going to do about it?" Of course, you never want to push it to that, because I don't work on movies with a budget of fifty million plus. I mostly work on movies where people have had to scrape money together. One doesn't want to make life harder for them than it already is.

CZ: Were you ever in a situation where you wanted more takes, where you said, "That didn't feel right to me"?

TC: I've never encountered a problem with getting extra takes if I felt them necessary.

CZ: Do you use rushes as a tool?

TC: Yes, I go to rushes, but that's changed a lot. What normally happened was at the end of the day's shooting, you all repaired to a theater somewhere and watched rushes. If you were in a studio, then you went to the screening and watched rushes. But now, everything's done on video, so there isn't that same situation, which I thought was really good. They still do it in France; actually, most people on the crew, sometimes even the drivers, come to watch rushes. That's terrific, because it means that everybody knows they're making the same movie, and that we're all in it together. Now, it's all so fragmented. You get handed a videotape, and take it to a trailer and watch it on a silly little television screen, so you can't see it properly anyway. A bad video transfer is not the same as film.

But it is good to view rushes, because it shows you a number of things. It shows, first of all, whether what you're doing is working, and how the guy's shooting it. And if there's anything you've got to look out for—if he's favoring this or that kind of thing. Is the Director of Photography a Prince of Darkness?

CZ: I take it you mean that a lot of the film is shot in shadows?

TC: Exactly.

CZ: Did you ever feel that a role affected you emotionally in any way, or is it always just a job?

TC: Yes, curiously, *Whose Life Is It Anyway?* did, but not consciously. I didn't ever feel depressed or down while doing it. But where it popped up was in dreams. I would dream that it had happened; that I was paralyzed, or that one of the family was paralyzed. It meant that something was festering away underneath, but not in my conscious life.

CZ: How do you get your creative juices flowing if they're not? Do you ever use improvisation as a tool?

TC: If a scene isn't working, it's because it's not written properly. That's why you start improvising. Because you know what the writer's trying to say, but he can't say it. So you start improvising and messing around with it to try and make it work. But it's not to get your own creative juices flowing, but to get the scene right.

CZ: Do you feel that you can go to a director and ask for help?

TC: Yes. I don't know how likely you'd be to get it. It's not often you get it, because many directors can't direct, as many actors can't act, and many writers can't write. Of course, there are some directors I would love to work with, like Sydney Pollock. I'd absolutely love to work with him. I'm sure with Sydney I'd say, "What do you think about this?" A delightful and highly intelligent man.

CZ: But didn't you say, not long ago, that you loathed and despised discussions of acting?

TC: It depends on how useful it is. One night in New York after a performance of *Whose Life Is It Anyway?*, I came out of the theater into a deserted street and was met by a girl. The conversation went something like this:

Girl: "Can I ask you a personal question?"

Tom Conti: [cautiously] "Yes."

G: "Would you tell me about the man with the gun?" I thought my number was up, that her significant other was hiding in a doorway about to dispatch me to the great green room in the sky.

TC: "What man with what gun?"

G: "In the play."

TC: "Have you seen the play?"

G: "Yes."

TC: "Well, there are no men with guns in this play."

G: "No, in your imagination."

TC: "What are you talking about?"

G: "In acting class, the teacher told us that every night you imagine that in the audience was a man with a gun pointed at you."

TC: "Why on earth would I do that?"

G: "To give yourself a feeling of impending death."

TC: "Leave your acting school immediately."

It's disgraceful, people filling youngsters' heads with complete bloody nonsense.

CZ: Obviously, the teacher was trying to stimulate their imaginations.

TC: Well, that's no good, that's stupid! I've no patience with drama schools. They should all be radically altered. We went through the whole thing—we did dancing, we did mime, we did improvisation, and this was to enrich our imaginations; to make them more powerful. And at the end of three years, the people with no imaginations still had no imaginations, despite years of living in the world, and three years of studying mime and threading needles. There is only one thing that works, and that is doing plays. That's the only thing that teaches you anything about acting. That and, of course, watching the world go by.

CZ: What technique are you referring to that you learned in drama school?

TC: What they taught you to do was to look at what you did. And that is the technique, so you know what you're doing. On the stage or on the screen, if you do that [moves foot], you should know that you did it. Nothing should be random about a performance, although it should look as if it is. If you do that [lifts hand], you do it for a reason.

CZ: So then you are examining text and saying, "Why am I doing this?"

TC: It all goes like lightning. The next time you might not do it that way. You have to think through it fresh, all the time, every second. A performance, whether it lasts thirty seconds of a take for a movie, or two hours on the stage, has got to be done with the same concentration as a driver of a Formula One racing car. That's how hard you have to think. When things get out of control, suddenly it's going very fast, and things go wrong, and when you are driving a racing car, you lose control and hit the tire wall. The moment you lose your concentration, it crumbles. I don't think that actors quite understand how much you have to think on the stage, and how much you have to be aware. You have to be aware of everything. You have to be aware of every cough in the audience so you can sidestep it if it's going to coincide with an important word; you have to put in a pause to get round it, or say a word twice, in a completely naturalistic fashion, so that it seems as if it was meant to be there. You have to be aware of what other people are doing; you have to be aware of every single thing. So that's what you have to teach actors: to think, listen, and look as if their lives depend on it.

CZ: I think we can establish that you're not an actor who wants to set a play.

TC: You kill it if you do that. And you kill all the actors. When you're in the third or fourth month of a run, and it becomes evident that one of the actors has gone onto automatic pilot, it's a good idea to change the verb tense of one of your lines, and if the verb tense in his subsequent line doesn't match yours, then you raise an eyebrow.

CZ: You once said, "A film set is just a never-ending hell." Can you talk about that? [laughter]

TC: I don't really believe that now. There are days when it can be. It must have been *American Dreamer* (1984), which was kind of a never-ending hell. Nobody was very happy, and it's very difficult to be funny when the set isn't happy. There is a kind of hell, because what everybody's trying to do is almost impossible. When you think about the number of elements that have to come together at the right time, and the number of departments that have to be satisfied: the director, the actors, the sound, the cameraman. For the most part, it's not hell. I think a lot of directors find it a never-ending hell. Those are the ones who come onto the set in the morning with their eyes a little bit wide with terror.

CZ: Your work on Merry Christmas, Mr. Lawrence *is one of your most well-known screen roles. How did you prepare yourself for that film, since you obviously had to learn some Japanese?*

TC: A lot of Japanese. Well, for that, we were on a little island in the middle of the Pacific. I had this New York Jewish guy who was the greatest linguist I've ever come across; he could speak about six languages; he was completely amazing. One of his languages was Japanese; he was completely fluent. We just walked on the beach all day, every day, for the ten days or so before we started shooting, with him bashing this Japanese into my head. By the end of it, I really knew it. Because you can't stumble. It'd be terrible if you had to do take after take.

On the first day, there was a long duologue between myself and Takeshi, who played the sergeant. He's a terrific actor, a comic [and film director]. I said to the director, Oshima, "Are you going to be doing this in sections?" thinking, "There's so much Japanese, I'll never get through it," and he said, "Mm." And I said, "What? You want to do it in one take?" He said, [grunts]. On the morning of the shooting, we did the scene in a "oner" and it worked. Oshima was happy, and it started me off well in the movie. The pressure was off, and from that moment I didn't worry about the Japanese because I knew we could get through it.

CZ: How else did you prepare yourself for working on the film, since you were playing a man who was supposed to have been in Japan since 1937, when there was a very anti-foreign, repressive regime. Did you do any reading about the subject?

TC: Of course, I was born at the beginning of the war, or just after the beginning, so all my reading, or a great deal of it, was books about the war. I knew about the war. I lived through it as a small boy—and you actually do get a great feeling of what it's like, even at that age. You know something immense is going on, but it's normal, because it's been happening your whole life. We read books about Japanese prisoner-of-war camps; we loved all that stuff. So there was nothing that I hadn't already read about when I started doing this picture.

CZ: How was it to work with Oshima?

TC: I loved it. It was so exciting; it was my second or third movie, but the other two had been some years before that, in the early seventies. But I'd worked in the theater for years and years, and on television. It was just exciting being in the movies, and being in such an exotic, foreign land. All of that is magical when you're an actor. I was no longer young by then, but still fairly new to movies, and Oshima was such an exotic character.

CZ: I imagine you got on well with Robert Altman—you worked with him twice, on The Dumbwaiter *and then* Beyond Therapy *(1987).*

TC: I loved that more than anything. I never enjoyed working with anyone like I enjoyed working with Bob. Because he does that best of all things—which we should all do—and that is to try to encourage people to fulfil their potential as whatever they are: cameraman, or actor, or what have you. He's encouraging, and hugely supportive, and he's great fun at dinner. What more could you want?

CZ: I understand he does a great deal of improvisation with his actors before shooting.

TC: Well, I didn't do that probably because both the films I did with him were originally stage plays. And the dialogue was very, very good in both of them, so it wasn't an improvisational set-up . . . despite what Harold thinks. [laughs]

CZ: Moving on to a more global arena: What do you think it is about the British that resists making heroes out of their actors?

TC: Well, the British are a kind of tortured nation. "Keep yourself part of the flock," "Don't stand out too much," "Keep yourself to yourself," and "Don't wave the flag," unless of course we're at war, then we wave it everywhere.

There's a reticence about the British that makes them self-effacing, talking themselves down. It happens all the time. We all do it. If I'm paid a compliment, I sort of squirm; I mean it's ridiculous. I'm actually better at it now. I just say, "Thank you very much." It embarrasses us for some reason. It has become more so. England has become a sort of socialist country despite Margaret Thatcher's great attempts at the contrary. For example, captains of industry never have a Rolls Royce or a Bentley. I have a Bentley, because I'm not a captain of industry. But still people think, "Son of a bitch . . . ." But I don't care. What are we to do with all the people who make Bentleys, should we just throw them in the Thames? Do you say, "We must stop doing work which is of a very high engineering standard." Quality is what we should all be aiming at. Very nice if everybody could drive a Bentley. I wouldn't object at all.

I always went to work in a suit and tie, because I felt that if there were people at the stage door when you came out, they didn't want you to look the same as they did; and they don't. That's the difference with America. Americans want to see their actors as something special. They want stars to be stars. And I think they actually also like that in England. They like it and they don't like it. They love to say, "Well, he's just one of the boys," when he's not actually. He's far from being "one of the boys."

CZ: What do you think makes actors into stars?

TC: Some actors are not going to be stars, because they're not. It's a weird thing, and it's not got to do with talent either. Stars aren't necessarily great actors. There are some stars who are great actors and they're fabulous to watch—like Nicholson or De Niro—just hugely talented stars. There's too much acting and a certain amount of narcissism in some of our actors that I don't really like; it isn't really to my taste.

CZ: It's implicit in your theory of acting that films have to be realistic.

TC: I think to be good, they do. To be a really proper cinema, it does have to be about realism. You have to completely believe it. I don't mean that you won't get away with it if you don't. That's what marks a really great performance, or a really great cinema: that it's so real that you're completely taken in by it.

But that's just personal taste. People say to others, "I love Tom Conti."And others will say, "How can you? It's so awful what he does!" That's just the way it is, there's nothing you can do about it. Some people like Giacometti, some people don't know what the hell he's on about.

CZ: Do you see yourself as a changed actor from the time of The Norman Conquests *(1978), for example?*

TC: Yes, I think I'm better at it now. You do improve with age, and knowledge of the world, and that's a very important thing about being an actor. I mean, it's always been said about the playing of Hamlet that you can't play it till you're forty, because you don't know what the hell it's all about. You don't know what life is about. Shakespeare actually wrote *Hamlet* as a character of great maturity, despite the fact that he's supposed to be in his twenties. I haven't seen a *Hamlet* since Olivier that has interested me, and he did that fifty years ago.

CZ: What do you think has been your greatest challenge as an actor?

TC: Not killing an actress with whom I once worked was probably the greatest challenge. Woody Allen's *Bullets Over Broadway* (1994) has the greatest solution to bad actors. Shoot them and drop them in the East River. Perfect. It's such a simple and wonderful solution. Just get rid of the buggers. The actress with whom I had a problem was young, intelligent, and a very nice girl. But she absolutely insisted on overacting dreadfully. And nothing would budge her.

CZ: Who are your great heroes—not necessarily from show business.

TC: Certainly a great number from the music world; I think a lot of Italian composers of opera—Bellini and Puccini are great heroes. Shostakovich is a great hero—a man of stunning and rainbow-spectrum ability. Obviously, the other ones, like Mozart and such. On performance, Toscanini, Glenn Gould—a complete and blazing light in my life. It's funny, people say that they know where they were when Kennedy died—

which I do—I also remember exactly where I was when I'd heard that Glenn Gould had died, and what I thought: "Oh Jesus, I can't believe it." And another pianist, called Arturo Benedetti Michelangeli. These are huge, stunning talents—Dino Lipatti, Beniamino Gigli. Of actors that I like to watch, De Niro, certainly, Hoffman. Hackman I think is just the most amazing actor. He never makes a mistake. Never. He was wonderful in *The Firm* (1993); there's a scene he has with Jeanne Tripplehorn towards the end of the movie when he confesses what his life is. He's great. And Walter Matthau was a complete joy to watch. I think the film I've seen more than any other is *The Sunshine Boys* (1975). My daughter and I watched it over and over. She's twenty-three now; we started watching it when she was about five. Completely wonderful.

There are some actresses in America I think are terrific. I think Julia Roberts is a hugely underrated talent. People don't realize how clever she is. Jessica Lange, Michelle Pfeiffer, Kim Basinger, Annette Bening, Meryl Streep. There's a long list of wonderful actresses.

Career Highlights

Film: *Galileo* 75. *The Haunting of Julia* 76. *Reuben, Reuben* (AAN, GGN) 82. *Merry Christmas, Mr. Lawrence* (New York Film Critics Award) 83. *Beyond Therapy* 87. *Someone Else's America* 95. *Out of Control* 98. *Something to Believe In* 98. *The Enemy* 2001.

Theater: *Savages* 73. *The Devil's Disciple* 76. *Don Juan* 76. *Whose Life Is It Anyway?* (Variety Club Award, Olivier, Tony) 78–79. *They're Playing Our Song* 80. *Romantic Comedy* 82. *The Italian Straw Hat* 86. *Jeffrey Bernard Is Unwell* 90. *The Ride Down Mt. Morgan* 91–92. *Present Laughter* 93. *Chapter Two* 96. *Otherwise Engaged* 96. *Art* 99. *The Last of the Red Hot Lovers* 99.

Television: *Madame Bovary* 75. *Glittering Prizes* 76. *The Norman Conquests* 78. *Blade on the Feather* 80. *Nazi Hunter: The Beate Klarsfeld Story* 86. *The Dumbwaiter* 87. *Fatal Judgment* 88. *Voices Within: The Lives of Truddi Chase* 90. Series: "The Wright Verdicts" 95. "Cinderella and Me" 2001.

James Fox

We can't just be talented artists, we have to be human beings.

CAROLE ZUCKER: Let's talk about the cultural influences that you had when you were growing up. You were born in 1939, so you were a child during the war years, and the postwar years, and an adolescent in the fifties. What sort of schooling did you have?

JAMES FOX: As far as schooling is concerned, I was at a boarding school in Sussex to start with, and then at a public school, Harrow, in North London. These were middle-class schools, so I was privileged to that extent. They were boarding schools, which meant they were single-sex schools. Socially, in my family, I come from pretty theatrical stock on both sides. My mother was an actress, my father's mother was an actress, my mother's father is a theater writer; my brothers, Edward and Robert, are in the business. Culturally, in terms of religion, probably not much more than nominal.

CZ: Did you go to movies or theater when you were growing up? You were an adolescent at a time when people like James Dean and Marlon Brando were first coming on the scene. Did they influence you at all?

JF: Yes, but you must remember, the time when I was in movies, as a kid, at eleven and twelve, we were still in the Rock Hudson, Doris Day era, and Hollywood musicals. So probably my local cinema wasn't showing these more modern interpretations. They were still stuck with some beautiful fifties movies: Crosby, Sinatra, and stuff like this, which was very influential, and lovely. The later, more serious stuff, I must have got toward the end of my adolescence, along with Elvis Presley in fifty-six, fifty-seven or so. Just around the time I was leaving school, American rock and roll music was a huge influence on me. More than my drama school, which was out of touch with the drama that I appreciated, anyway.

CZ: Where did you go to drama school?

JF: The Central School of Speech and Drama.

CZ: And Edward went to RADA. Why did you choose Central and not RADA?

JF: I don't remember why. I thought RADA was probably too good, or that I wouldn't get in, or something. Having left school a good year and a half before the end of the full course, in other words, before I was eighteen years old, my parents must have said, "You've got to go and continue some kind of training and if you want to go into the acting world, you must go to drama school and continue to be a student." Unfortunately, compulsory military service interrupted that, but I left school even before that compulsory military service to get practical experience in the theater. I was no kind of a student.

CZ: Do you feel that you took anything away from Central School that you still use?

JF: Nothing that I use, just a little envy of all the really bright students like Judi Dench and Vanessa Redgrave, who were very talented, as well as good students.

CZ: Did anyone encourage you to be an actor?

JF: I don't think they did, no. My feeling for it was pretty instinctive.

CZ: When did you realize that you had talent?

JF: I suppose when I did the films at the age of eleven, I must have been conscious of the affirmation and approval; there must have been a certain facility that I felt.

CZ: Was it fun for you to act as a young boy?

JF: It was a lot of fun. For an individualist like myself, acting is a satisfying thing to indulge in. I'm very intuitive and visual, and so everything that came to me was exciting, and novel and refreshing, compared to anything academic or more literal.

CZ: Can you talk about The Servant *(1963), which was really the beginning of your career as an adult? I found it unusual that you were chosen for that role, since you didn't have very much experience, and you were being pitted against Dirk Bogarde, who was quite experienced. Perhaps on some subtextual level, that's what the film is about.*

JF: Well, that was a time when people were taking gambles on unknown talent. Also, as you're saying, the role demanded a relatively young, inexperienced person, and if the more professional acting talent had been cast, the film would have lost its critique of class. I had just completed my National Service in a rather smart regiment, so I had been exposed to that milieu of rich and privileged people; I was living and walking around a bit like that anyway. I had the necessary acting connections or qualities that they thought were right. Joe Losey did test me for it, so he knew what I was able to do and how I looked on camera. I think it was a great stroke of luck that I got it. I just happened to be going out with Sarah Miles, who was picked for the role of Vera, and they weren't finding it easy to get the money for the film. When they got Sarah, who was at that time quite hot, they managed to put together the last bit of financing.

*CZ: You talked in your autobiography [*Comeback: An Actor's Direction*] about taking some acting lessons with Vivian Matalon. They sound like they were based on Stanislavski's teachings. Did you feel inspired by your work with him to read Stanislavski?*

JF: Yes, I read Stanislavski, but I found it difficult to connect those ideas with my own personal experience. But I could see many of the principles. What was good was that Vivian had absorbed Stanislavski and Lee Strasberg, and had been an actor, and had already become a director. So he had distilled quite a lot of things for himself, and rather than talk theory, we always talked about the practical apects of scenes. Whatever we did was in relation to the work. Everything I've learned about acting, I learned from Vivian, and absorbing it from others.

CZ: You make an interesting statement in your book that "The character of Tony was very close to my own experience and temperament, but I still

*needed to know how to communicate that." Can you explain that? That
gap between understanding something and communicating it.*

JF: I think that is the essence of acting. It was particularly clear to me in *Performance* (1970), a film I did later, where I was cast well away from the role
of Tony in *The Servant*. When I made *The Servant*, I wasn't rich, I wasn't a
homeowner, I wasn't in the strange kind of business world that Tony was in,
and I would never in a million years think of having a servant. It was very
far from the world I lived in. There was so much distance to go, really, from
where I was living. But that was much closer than the world of *Performance*.

The great actors are the ones who know how to get it to the audience,
how to sell it. In a very limited way, I can do that. But the great actors
are the ones who make the audience do the work, because they have the
trick of not only understanding what they're doing, but knowing how
they want it to impact on the receiver. Acting is a totally receiver-oriented
business, and hammy acting is enjoyably missing it, but going for it in a
big way. It just misses the target.

*CZ: You also talk about how you worked on simple intentions for each
scene, and you mention subtext, and interior dialogue. Can you think of
some examples of how you've used those things either in* The Servant *or in
something that you've done more recently?*

JF: Vivian totally believed in the Stanislavski method—that acting is not
about demonstrating. It's about an action, a simple thing. Everything we
do in life is motivated by the need to do something to carry out a purpose
or intention; even if you're on the receiving end of a reprimand, you have
an intention, there's something that you're trying to do. I can't literally
jump back into *The Servant*, but we would break down every single scene.
A very simple scene at the beginning of *The Servant* is my interviewing
Barrett [Dirk Bogarde], and I imagined the activity, and the motivation of
the character, Tony. The actor must explore a range of choices and put in
as much information as they can, in the preparatory stage. In those days,
at the age of twenty-four, I would have thought, "Do I like him; therefore,
do I want him to like me? Can he do his job?" What sort of action do you
do for that? Well, I suppose you could say, "I will try to put him at ease as
much as possible so he can be himself." How do I do that? Sit him down,
speak to him in a friendlyish tone. These kinds of choices and imaginative

exercises stem from an action. An interview would be one action. There were other actions in the film to do with two different women: one who my character was trying to continue a normal relationship with, which wasn't very exciting, and one that was very exciting, illicit, and dangerous. The acting choices would have involved the same questions: "What am I trying to do with this person? Why am I trying to do it? What do I want to get from this situation? How do I deal with it from the things they're trying to get from me? Where do I want to end up at the end of this scene? Have I succeeded? How do I feel about that? Could I have done it differently?" Vivian stimulated all my thinking in this way, and because of my temperament—which is that I am a slow thinker, and a slow and deliberate reasoner in some ways—I feel more safe on that ground of analysis and thoughtful preparation. That acting suits me, because with a text in front of me, I can start asking these questions in a leisurely way of myself, maybe as the dramatist did as they created the text.

CZ: Why do you think that you were more receptive to lessons about acting with Vivian Matalon than you were when you went to the Central School?

JF: Because they didn't have that sort of program. They never had any intelligent and analytical approach, and after all, we were living in a psychoanalytic world by that time.

CZ: As far as I can tell, they've changed their focus somewhat from the time when you were there. They now have teachers from The Drama Centre who teach there, and their work is primarily based on the teachings of Stanislavski.

JF: I heard that The Drama Centre is one of these schools that teaches that actors almost need to be broken down, which is rather disturbing. It worries me greatly. In fact, I think actors need building up, and you can only arrive as an actor with whatever is in your closet, in your store cupboard. To try to destroy or take away that is to put you through an exercise that is totally meaningless. To me, actors work from confidence and love, and they work from whatever needs to be elicited, or drawn from them, by intelligent questions in a positive atmosphere.

I can say that actors have given stunning performances even under fear, and there's no question that fear can create something, but it certainly doesn't create a happy actor. I think these methods are wrong, rather like a musician who is unable to play a tortured or tormented piece of music unless they were in control of their instrument, and allow their imagination to play through their interpretation. I find the analogy exactly the same; you could never control your instrument effectively with relaxation and technique if you were in some kind of torment. It's the same with the actor's instrument. I find that those theories are wrong. But, who am I to say, because I haven't tested it against a hundred cases. What do you think?

CZ: I think the idea is to break down your inhibitions so that emotions are able to flow through you, and you can relate freely to a given text and character. But it doesn't work for everybody. Some students grow emotionally and psychologically out of that experience, or they work very hard and well, because they're being pressured.

JF: Yes, I'm sure, that is probably how you grow, when there is pressure.

CZ: The sixties must have been a very heady time for you. What was it like to cope with this rather large amount of international fame, since you were also doing popular international films like Those Magnificent Men in Their Flying Machines *(1965) and* Thoroughly Modern Millie *(1967)?*

JF: How did I cope with it? I don't know. The sixties were an overload, but for me it was nice to get an education outside school, and it was the beginning of that process. A major influence in my life was a teacher I write about in my book, who began to take me a little bit more seriously than anyone else had in terms of my creative ability, and also my capacity for friendship, which I needed terrifically. This man had a very good influence on me, introducing me to classical music, literature, and theater of a much more interesting nature than the kind I was exposed to at Central. Through him, I saw Beckett, and Pinter, and Osborne, and read the poets, and listened to music, and just got more of an education.

But the classroom was pop music and drugs and travel and American movies, and all these tremendously mind-enlarging experiences. They were just stimulating times, and I don't know whether it rubbed off on my work as well. It's just growing up in my twenties, and I was very fortunate, and did a lot of enjoyable things.

CZ: When you went to the United States and did The Chase *(1965), you were working with an almost entirely "method" cast and director, Arthur Penn. What was that experience like for you?*

JF: It was superb, but I think Arthur Penn may have got a little bit irritated with me. He worked in a way rather like Vivian, but I remember he wanted to improvise more. I have never been a fan of improvisation, which to me is not a meaningful exercise. Arthur did try to do that with Jane Fonda and myself, and I don't think I was the best side of it, but I was so respectful of the company of actors; it was just awe-inspiring. Of course, by then they were very, very mature and experienced professionals as well, so we never talked about acting; I just watched them and admired them. In fact, it's an incredible cast, isn't it? Marlon Brando, Robert Duvall, Robert Redford, and Jane Fonda, and Richard Bradford, and Janice Rule. They're the finest actors of their generation.

That film is the equivalent of *Twelve Angry Men* (1957), in terms of acting talent and experience. *Twelve Angry Men* is the kind of film that influenced me more than any other. It's where I most clearly saw the connection between great communicating, great text, and great thinking and preparation and casting. I would have loved to have worked with Lumet. Penn, Lumet, and Kazan were the heroes of the day. What better? Now we're living in a much more devalued society, where their kind of work can't even get a hearing, and we're all the poorer for it, so we have to find our pleasures somewhere other than the cinema, very often.

CZ: I agree that mainstream filmmaking is pretty sad right now; I'm hoping it is just a bad period. Is there something for you that's inherent in British performance, or to the British temperament, that results in certain types of acting? Judi Dench referred to Peggy Ashcroft as the quintessential British actor. It seems that British actors are uninterested in calling themselves "artists"; they'd rather say, "I'm doing my job." I wonder where that comes from?

JF: Yeah, I wonder where it does. We find we're ashamed to take ourselves seriously, because we're not taken seriously by our peers and by our media.

CZ: Do you think that's true?

JF: Yes. We're not living in a very cultured society here, so actors have inferiority feelings about what they do. This is possibly why we've produced some very good ones, because they're so determined to show that what they do is good that they become very proficient at it. Peggy would have played the great European classical roles as well as Shakespeare, and

I never thought of her as being particularly British, because she never came on with a particular class or attitude; she had a liberal intelligence, which I think is quite universal, and that's why she was able to play the classics. If being quintessentially British means a modesty, and a desire to be a real human being, as well as an actress, which, to me, is the whole point, then I think that may be rather British—realizing that life and the work must go hand in hand for it to be a growing experience. I think that is something that American actors rightly admire. I think Judi and Peggy both exemplify that; they're richly gifted human beings, they're determined to be human and to keep growing and living as well as portraying. And they have a right modesty about their place; they know that they're inflated by society and by the culture which adores them. We need them, because otherwise we'd listen to all this other rubbish and think that was where it's at. That's not where it's at all. [laughs]

CZ: What do you find different about working in "art" films and films that are strictly entertainment, or do you not make a distinction between the two? I find in your career that you move between the two all the time, like The Remains of the Day *(1993),* Fall from Grace *(1994),* The Servant, A Question of Attribution *(1992) and then, on the other side,* Thoroughly Modern Millie *and a television series like "The Choir" (1995).*

JF: I'd love to be able to answer that, or know what the difference is. I always think that if you can blend commerciality with a rich experience, that would be like a symphony that communicates strongly. An art film would be a bit more like chamber music, perhaps: a little harder, a little more inaccessible, but very richly rewarding if you're willing to give it the effort, if you want to learn about something. Well, both are valid. What I don't like to be in, and would love to avoid being in, is crap. There's just so much of that that it's very difficult to avoid being in it as you try and earn your living.

CZ: Do you feel, on the whole, that directors have been helpful to you?

JF: I have been fortunate, because I always try to work with directors I feel a sympathy with. I have obviously lost out, but in the fifty or so things I have done, I must have really scored forty times out of fifty, with some decent people. I've seldom been at war with a director, because I think directors are the crucial people, apart from the writers. What a thing to be a director! If you're an inspiring human being who understands, and who can communicate, and who has the breadth and ability to lead, it's inspiring for an actor to be with a great director. A great director is everything, and I have really been fortunate. So far in my career, I've worked with some of the best directors of our times, and it has been completely what has made my career successful—the only thing, really, I'd say. It's just their ability to be able to use me, and for me to be able to have the honor of being a part of what they wanted to say about a particular thing. I can't understand why anyone would want to be an actor and not work with the best directors; that, to me, is the whole point.

CZ: Some directors say that the thing they enjoy least is working with actors; they enjoy editing, and postproduction and preproduction.

JF: I know, I know. Well, David Lean was reputed to be one of those, but I didn't think that was true. He could be unpleasant, but I've heard so many great actors' stories about him, and he adored people like Celia Johnson, William Holden, Jack Hawkins, and Charles Laughton. He adored the good actors. He probably found actors rather vain and silly and childish. In certain respects they are, I mean, they are rather a silly bunch of egotistical people. There are a lot of bad actors, but don't hate all actors because of the bad ones.

CZ: Can we talk about Performance? *It was a big favorite in the drug scene in the late sixties and early seventies.*

JF: It was a trip, wasn't it? It was a really weird experience. It was sex and violence, and it was bizarre.

CZ: I think it holds up now, even thirty years later.

JF: It's a very good film, and it takes you where you probably hadn't been yourself, and were quite intrigued to go.

CZ: I found it surprizing that you said that the role of Chas was written for you.

JF: Well, I was very friendly with Donald Cammell, the film's co-director.

CZ: Can you talk about how you prepared for the part? I know that you did a lot of research, because the role was something so different from anything you'd done previously.

JF: I think that probably when Donald wrote the part of Chas, there were two things he was trying to do: one was trying to show something about the background to the London underworld, the gangster world which was being influenced by the American mafia and big business coming into the underworld; and the other thing he wanted to show was the rock-and-roll world, and he needed an actor to cross over into the rock-and-roll world and go through this kind of experience. He must have thought, "Well, I need an actor who can do both those things." Maybe I could connect more with the second experience. But, fortunately, I connected with the first experience as well, through being kicked out of the nest, really. I mean, Donald and Nic Roeg said, "We're in the preproduction stage, it's very tight, you can't mess around us all day, we're preparing a film here. You've got to go away and become this part. So go away, we don't want to see you again for another six weeks." I found that very frightening, and rather exciting and challenging, so I went shopping for clothes, where the gangsters buy their clothes, and I changed my identity. Then I started to hang out as the character that I was creating and inventing, where these gangsters were living, in Southeast London.

CZ: Was it frightening for you at all?

JF: No, it was very exciting. I never got to the higher echelons, because they wouldn't have wanted to be connected with some movie. But I certainly mixed with some of the "talent" there, and I just absorbed it. They must have found me quite bizarre, really, coming around as an actor. That would have been part of my Stanislavskian training. Here was a huge gap to try and bridge, and I had to get totally immersed in it to even begin to make sense of it, apart from imitating the way these people spoke, which was handy in the sense that, obviously, I do have a reasonably good ear. I'm a person who absorbs it through the pores of my skin as well, and I did that before these techniques were common. It was an exciting adventure for me, and it's not one I would want to go through too often.

I don't think people have credited me, or the film *Performance*, with the ability to tell the audience what we wanted to tell them. We knew what we were doing. I'm always depicted as a rather druggy person who went through a nervous breakdown and became a religious maniac because of that film. This is so far from the truth as to be ridiculous; we were professional people making a film. We were absorbing every influence we possibly could, but there was always that ability to sell it, to tell it, and I don't think people want to hear that. They can't hear it, perhaps.

CZ: You said in the interview that if your mind was blown, it was blown a long time before Performance.

JF: I think in my living, I had taken all the drugs and had all the experiences that the film might have been purporting to represent, but you cannot do that on film with cameras turning, or you end up with a film like *Easy Rider* (1969), which is rather a self-consciously dreadful film. Although it's fascinating, to me it is rather a bad film as well, because you can see the actors are stoned, and you feel like saying, "Well, please, don't be stoned on me." I know the audiences found that intriguing, but I think there is a difference.

CZ: What do you think that Chas found when he got to the house in Notting Hill?

JF: He found a situation that he regarded as rather disgusting, and he recognized it in the character of Turner [Mick Jagger]. I think this was what made it hard for me, because I was, of course, much, much closer emotionally and socially to where that house, where that ménage was, than I was to Chas. So the question I had to keep in mind was "How would this boy feel about these druggy, decadent rock people?" That was quite an acting challenge, because I had to play it not only through myself, but through what I thought Chas would be. I had to say, "Okay, so what do you feel about these people taking drugs?" Well, I think Chas thought they were degenerates, but, at the same time, he had one overriding purpose and intention, which was always that if they didn't help him, he wasn't going to get out of the country. And he was also very ill; he had been very badly beaten, so always his intention was survival. Anyway, you can't cope with drugs; if you're taking drugs, they will have an effect on you as you have that experience, so he went through all their little games and stuff. His intention would have been "I have got to try and keep some kind of a cool head until I get the photographs and the disguise I need to get out of here," and also "Am I going to have to kill them when I go?" I think he would have thought they were rather harmless, pathetic people with too much money, too little idea about life, and he would have rather despised them.

Actually, they were probably more interesting than he was, and they were rather impressed with him, because he was still virile as a "performer" and they, through drugs and introspection, had become impotent. So there's something rather touching about him and all that was explored. My job as an actor was to say, "These are a bunch of degenerates, and I need to get out of here." It's very simple!

CZ: You've said that Mick Jagger didn't really take acting very seriously. You were making a great effort to submerge yourself in this role, yet he didn't care much. Did that effect you?

JF: Looking at it now, I think it was a wonderful performance. The fact that he didn't take it seriously was completely right for Turner; he didn't take anything seriously anyway. He was frivolous and casual, and yet, like Turner, he was also scared and intrigued. Mick never wanted to go through the processes that I go through as an actor.

CZ: Did you ever discuss any of the homoerotic elements in the film, because that struck me quite strongly as I watched the film this time—the milieu of Harry Flowers and all the "boys" that surround him; your relationship with Jagger; the fact that you choose to sleep with a woman who looks very much like a boy, rather than sleeping with the much more feminine Anita Pallenberg, who clearly offers herself to you. In the scene when the gangster, your former friend, Tony, comes smashing into your apartment, he pulls down your trousers and screams at you over and over, "Say I'm a . . ." and he never finishes the sentence. It obviously makes you angry enough to kill him. Did you ever talk about that?

JF: The homoeroticism of the film. . . . Never talked about it; I'm inhibited about it, and I think that if he had been homosexual, it is never explored beyond innuendo.

CZ: But it's certainly very present in the film.

JF: It's strongly there, and I don't have any problem with that, and if the suggestion had been made to me at the time, I don't know how I would have related to it. As I say, I was rather squeamish about showing any homosexual side; there was a small sequence when Jagger and Chas are in bed together, with the Michelle Breton character. There's no doubt that the Krays did have that in their gang; there's a culture of male bonding and macho behavior that males appreciate. And there's an inference that Chas might have had a relationship with Tony, the guy he kills, when they were in the nick [prison], or when they were kids. It's in the past, but it niggles, so when he brings it up, Chas gets mad.

CZ: There are also strong homoerotic undertones in The Servant, *as well.*

JF: The suggestion is there, too, so I think people have probably cast me in that kind of role. But *Performance* has it strongly; that's why it's so intriguing to a young audience.

CZ: It probably appeals to people who are looking for their identity, because essentially, that's what the film is about.

JF: Exactly, exactly.

CZ: You've also talked about how you became confused between acting and real life. Did you find that you were the sort of actor who took your roles home with you?

JF: No, I don't think so. I think the confusion between acting and real life happened around the time of my Christian conversion. Tensions that had been building up before and after. I don't know how to describe this, but the most recent impression that's hit me is a designer called Ossie Clark who's just died, who's about my age, and he was quite a brilliant artist and fashion designer of women's clothes in the sixties. I never met him, but once his day was over, he kind of declined. He went into drink and drugs, and then became very antisocial, and tried to revive his business, and died tragically, alone, very recently. As I look at him, I think, "That's the way I would have gone if my day had passed." I didn't have anything to connect me to reality, to learn from, to get values from. Who are you? I've been trying to address these issues for the last twenty-five years. In my twenties, I was typically not aware of those questions. I was living very much for my work, and in a more imaginative world. So reality is what Ossie Clark obviously either hated or never wanted to come to terms with. But you have to come to terms with it because that's our pilgrimage, that's our course. We've got to learn to cope with life; we have to grow as human beings. We can't just be talented artists, we have to be human beings, and being a human being is accepting all kinds of rather mundane and necessary things, and responsibilities. That is part of living, and I didn't grow up with that. Growing up in a theatrical family, I was maybe very willful, or nobody could ever reach me with these kind of lessons. I got to a stage where I felt, "I'll need this. I need it; if I don't have it, I'm screwed. I don't really want to be screwed, but I don't know how to have it."

There's something about reality that I find rather painful, actually. Things that are pure pleasure are not what I call reality, and yet they're probably the most real things in my life—that's the paradox. I think that probably the trick, for me, in acting, and why reality isn't as good, is that I don't feel that I am significant in any other way, but I feel a significance in communicating. I think everybody's searching for a significance, aren't they? And they find it in different ways. To me, acting connects me with significance. It's probably terribly vain, because the amount of experience that I can impart is actually tiny and inconsequential, compared to what another person might impart, but to me, it's significant, and if it's significant to me, then I can communicate it. Of course, that's why a bad or a cruel director is a nightmare, because they deny you your significance and destroy the one authentic moment that you might actually have to give them something or give an audience something. You deny that to a vulnerable person who's searching for appropriateness, and connection, and you can really damage something.

I think everybody's gifted, and actors should know whether they have a gift or not, but I think it's that vanity of significance, which probably isn't a vanity; it's probably a necessary experience for all artists: "Do I matter? Does it matter that I say something? Yes, it does. I do matter."

CZ: Do you think that's why you came back to acting after your conversion? Was it the quest for significance and communication that inspired you to come back to performing?

JF: Probably; that was the subtext. There must have been a desire to communicate something. A feeling of loss without doing that, if you like. But on a more prosaic level, I must have thought, "Well, I'm not doing the other thing terribly well, or gratifyingly, and I have a responsibility, I must try and earn a living." There's a survival instinct as well.

CZ: Do you feel that your embrace of Christianity has impacted on your acting at all?

JF: I wouldn't know how to answer that. It may have extended my range. I don't know that I would have been able to play "The Choir," but I don't know that it matters whether I play "The Choir" or not, do you know what I mean? [laughs] I don't know. I think that your value system, if it is rooted in something as wonderfully human as faith in God and Christ, something wonderfully real and human, should connect you with all kinds of things. It should open you up, gradually. I think it has affected me, and my acting, and I don't know how.

CZ: I see a willingness to challenge yourself in your career, to take on different kinds of roles. I'm thinking about films like Absolute Beginners *(1986) where you worked with a first-time director, and* A Question of Attribution, *or* As You Like It *(1992), working in theater after not performing on stage for a long time. Is that a deliberate quest?*

JF: I find that a really tough question.

CZ: Do you ever feel frustrated by being typecast as a stuffy Brit?

JF: They're probably connected, those two questions.

CZ: Yes, exactly, on the one hand, you really want to stretch yourself, and on the other hand, you often seem typecast in the same sorts of roles.

JF: I think this is where you'll have to become an interpreter, rather than a recorder, because you probably will make those connections, and I'm sure others will. The desire to break out from whatever you're perceived to be, and to give yourself challenges, is part of it. Sometimes, the roles I've played were of necessity, at times they were a challenge, and other times, I wanted to say something through them. I think I've always been a risk-taker; I like to leap and see where I land, and if it's worth it, if the experience is valuable, I'll go for it.

CZ: You said that one of your favorite films that you've done recently is The Remains of the Day. *How did you work on the character of Lord Darlington? I assume you read Ishugoro's book?*

JF: Yes.

CZ: Did you read material on British fascist sympathizers, like Sir Oswald Moseley, or books around that history?

JF: I'd obviously absorbed quite a lot of right-wing British attitudes in my education and background and social life, so I felt I knew where British fascist ideas were coming from: They're everywhere around in society today, so there's nothing new there. A lot of that was instinctive.

CZ: In thinking about Lord Darlington, I wondered: "Is he an honorable fool, an elitist with fascist tendencies, a traitor, an anti-Semite, or a dinosaur?"

JF: I think one critic put it very eloquently when he says that you can say all that about Lord Darlington, and you still end up with a few more questions. I like that about him. Harold Pinter cast me, because he wrote the original script, and said to Jim Ivory, "Would you have James; I think he'd be the ideal person." Jim Ivory obviously had to make his own decision on that, and took a long time to do it. He could have cast another person, and you would have had another reading. But I think Harold was right; I think that Kazuo Ishuguro did have someone in mind, similar to the way I ended up playing that part. Hopefully, we gave something of that interwar political motivation when Britain had declined from its position of Empire, but a person like Darlington's father would probably have been viceroy of India or something. Therefore, he'd inherited all the desire, and the zeal, and the authority, if you like, to try and make a world order and have peace. But he was weak, and he was influenced by some very bad people. He probably knew they were bad, but on the other hand, his motivation was his friendship; he was motivated by personal loyalty to some very nasty people. To me, it's a brilliant story of somebody who really wanted to do good and was completely out of their depth, that got in with a very bad crowd of people, got on the tiger instead of on the elephant, and got eaten alive. But this is terrific, because that's exactly what politics is like, don't you think? And Darlington was a naïf. He was also someone from Empire, and we can imagine what it was like to rule a third of the world like Britain did after the First World War.

CZ: I gather from what you're saying that you had a lot of sympathy for him, even though you thought that some of his actions were monstrous.

JF: Yes. As an English person, I have sympathy with my grandfather's generation. They went through a terrible transition, and it was a terrible price to pay, for them and for the people they dominated; that's why people shouldn't have Empires.

CZ: A Question of Attribution is a wonderful portrayal of Anthony Blunt, and a great script by Alan Bennett. You were playing a villain again, but a very sympathetic villain. Did you do a lot of research into his life and circle? Did you watch tapes of him to get the stance and the particularities of his diction.

JF: Yes, absolutely.

CZ: He's a very erudite and interesting person.

JF: Yes. I love that about him.

CZ: Did you respect him?

JF: Well, I did rather, yes. It's rather like in E. M. Forster, you know, I wouldn't betray my best friend, but I'd betray my country. That was a fashionable view in the twenties, for the very reasons that we've just been talking about with *The Remains of the Day*. I really rather admired Blunt, that he really believed that Communism was better, and he wanted to do everything he could to destroy countries that were anti-Communist, like his own. At the same time, he would understand art in such an elegant way. He was a very ambiguous, dangerous character, and I rather loved him. I love ambiguity, I guess.

CZ: How much do you rely on instinct and intuition? Has there been a moment that you can remember when you were acting when something wonderful happened on the spot, that you'd never thought of before?

JF: There must be dozens. Often it happens in collaboration. For instance in a recent film, we were doing a scene with Bernard Rose [the director], where Karenina asks Anna for the love letters that she's had from Vronski. In the book, there is a line where he says something to the effect of "You're denying me my conjugal rights, but you're having this affair with this appalling man." Bernard turned this almost into a rape, because the husband is so angry at his wife being violated by this other man, and denying him sexual relations, that he goes mad and tries to force her to have sex. Now this may well go beyond Tolstoy, but it was a most fabulous collaboration between actors and director and text, saying, "Well, maybe Tolstoy couldn't say that, but maybe that's exactly what was going on, or what they would have felt," and suddenly the text began to accommodate this fury, and jealousy, and passion. We turned it into a terrible moment of taking sex—and he couldn't, of course; she resisted him, and he was ashamed—but it was a wonderful moment where something happened that day that was totally unexpected. The best things are collaborative like that.

Career Highlights

Film: *The Servant* (BAFTA) 63. *King Rat* 65. *The Chase* 66. *Isadora* 68. *Performance* 70. *A Passage to India* (BAFTAN) 84. *Absolute Beginners* 86. *The Whistle Blower* 86. *The Russia House* 90. *Patriot Games* 92. *The Remains of the Day* 93. *Anna Karenina* 97. *Jinnah* 98. *The Golden Bowl* 2000. *Sexy Beast* 2000. *Up At the Villa* 2000.

Theater: *Uncle Vanya* 95.

Television: (Mini-Series and Made-for-Television Movies) *Nancy Astor* 84. *Shadow on the Sun* 88. "A Perfect Hero" 92. *A Question of Attribution* 92. *Heart of Darkness* 94. "The Old Curiosity Shop" 94. *Fall from Grace* 94. "The Choir" 95. *Gulliver's Travels* 96. "Metropolis" 2000.

Kerry Fox

I try and work with people that open you up in some way
. . . to only do projects that will change me.

CAROLE ZUCKER: You grew up in New Zealand. Can you describe your
family background and the cultural climate when you were growing up in
the seventies?

KERRY FOX: Well, I came from absolute suburbia, a new development. My
parents first moved there when they were married. At the back of our
place, even though we were in the middle of suburbia, it was all bush. In
the time I was there, all that got bulldozed down and became scrub and
gorse and stuff like that. New Zealand at that time was a really wealthy
place, with a social welfare state, so that all education, all health care, was
free, so there was the possibility to do anything. The quality of education
was really high, and it was expected that someone like me would go to
university and achieve whatever they wanted in life. That was the atmosphere when I was at school. And then, when I went to university at sev-
enteen, it was the beginning of the yuppie generation and money.

CZ: What university did you go to?

KF: Victoria University in Wellington. It was a big change for me. It
wasn't what I'd expected, because when my brother and sisters had gone
to university, it had been wild, and adventurous, and political, and artistic. When I went there, it was all about money, so I was really disappointed and left.

CZ: When did you become interested in performing?

KF: I started drama classes when I was six because my sisters went, and I begged to go. I asked the teacher, Heather Salmon, if I could go, and then I begged her for private lessons, because that seemed like the ideal thing. She was a great, fantastic teacher. She taught me until I was about twenty-one.

CZ: You went to a formal drama school as well, didn't you?

KF: That's The New Zealand Drama School, or that's what it was called when I went. At that time, they still had the policy of taking a token minority, one Maori, per year. After I left drama school, it changed a lot. The whole atmosphere of New Zealand was changing, culturally. When I was younger, I remember a theater in town called The Depot, which was attached to one of the main state-supported theaters. Then The Depot went out on its own, and started to do only new New Zealand works, which was a shocking thing at the time. You thought, "How could it ever survive? It'll never work." Then The Depot started to do only Maori work; it's now called Taki Rua.

CZ: Did you act there?

KF: Yeah, I did, a late-night show. But I stage-managed and did the lighting there for a bit; that's what I did after I left drama school. I was also part of the group of people who re-opened another theater. We did a few productions; it was aimed at bringing young people back into the theatre. That's still going; they're always doing new pieces of work. It's pretty erratic in terms of quality, but it's very much alive and pumping stuff out, and all new. It's called Bats Theatre.

CZ: Is there a big established theater in Wellington?

KF: Yeah, there were two main theaters when I was growing up. Circa Theatre, which is just over twenty years old now, and was new and fresh when it started. And there was The Downstage, which was the establishment, blue-rinse set theatre. It was always an event to go to the theater; my mother would take us.

My mother introduced us to ideas, and theater, plays, writing, and poetry. My parents loved books, and they encouraged us to read a lot.

They thought that reading was the source of everything, and if you were a prolific reader, it opened opportunities for you.

CZ: In what ways do you think your drama teacher influenced you?

KF: She taught me many things, but the basic thing was about communication. That was her aim and her focus, to encourage people to communicate with each other, and to listen and understand each other and to be able to express themselves. And she instilled a sense of New Zealand identity in me, because we learned a lot about New Zealand writers and new works; she was really forward-thinking. At that time, for a lot of people who did speech and drama, it was all Trinity-based [referring to the Dublin University]. She was one of the group of people who created the New Zealand Speech and Drama Association, whose focus was New Zealand work, in theatre, prose, and poetry.

CZ: What was the orientation of the drama school that you went to? How did they work on characterization and that sort of thing?

KF: We had a great mad queen as the Head of Drama. He was in his last term, and we had a really great year. We were a very close-knit group, twelve of us. We were strong together, and we're still close. We had a great time. We were eager to learn and helped each other a lot. And I think, for me, the basis of it was that you can't teach anyone to act. You can give them tools or ideas and help them along and support them, but you can't actually teach them to act. And that nobody's ever going to employ you, which is true in New Zealand. In a community that size, there are very, very few people who survive on acting alone.

CZ: Can you go into more detail about the orientation of the school?

KF: Our training was really just about the skills. We felt responsible for building a New Zealand cultural identity, which you can see when you look at New Zealand literature; it's all about identity. The basis of New Zealand culture is that it's at the end of the fuckin' world; and it's isolated, and each person is isolated. You know, the great books of New Zealand history are things like *Man Alone*, Janet Frame's book *To The Island*; they're always about being alone and making it through alone. That is the nature of the culture. And it's all new—everything there is new. People don't know how long New Zealand has been populated; maybe fifteen hundred years, maybe only seven hundred years, which is quite a big difference. And there's also the huge conflicts which have been brewing and bubbling and trying to be resolved over the last ten years, since I've been at drama school. New Zealand has changed so much since I left. When we were at drama school, we had our one token Maori person in the class, whereas now, fifty percent of the intake are Maori or Polynesian; it's really vital, and there's a lot of emphasis on Maori work and culture and language. The Maori language was nearly killed off. I remember when Mum went to school, people weren't allowed to speak Maori at school, something like the Irish situation. So there's this growth of Maori culture, and appreciation of it. For me, the little that I know is still part of me.

I'm not English, I never had this desire to come "home," to come here, and I feel torn. The word for me, what I am, is a Pakeha, which is a derogatory term for a "non-Maori" foreigner living in New Zealand. It's my race, in a way. I don't feel like I'm English, although I look English and I can pretend to be English, but I'm a New Zealander, and I'm a Caucasian New Zealander. I take comfort from the richness of the New Zealand culture, which is an incorporation of the bonding between the different cultures in New Zealand. Which I think is easier than in Australia, because there aren't so many cultures in New Zealand as there are in Australia. There are two main ones—Maori and English—those form the root.

CZ: Going back to your own performing style, was there any orientation towards Stanislavski, when you went to drama school?

KF: We were really dependent upon people coming in. Our drama teacher, this guy called Grant Tilly, is a really good actor; he can be a good teacher and he can be a terrible teacher. We'd get people coming in from foreign countries, or overseas; they'd come in and drop their pearls of wisdom about teaching, and Grant would say, "If only I spoke with a German accent, you'd all believe what I said," because he'd be saying the same thing, but we'd all say [starry-eyed], "God, he just said that we have to be honest to each other," and Grant would say, "How many times have I told you the same thing"? The biggest thing was being told that your only responsibility as an actor is to make the other actor look good.

CZ: So the aim was to work off the other person.

KF: Yeah, or working for them. They'd offer us many different techniques and styles. We did study Stanislavski; we did those exercises. We studied Growtowski; there was a man in New Zealand who'd studied

with him who came in and taught. So we had many, many different opportunities; there was no one philosophy. I believe that actors work in
many different ways all the time; there's no right or wrong—well, sometimes there's wrong, but that means that they're not very good anyway.
But we were given many possibilities; we were exposed to as much as
possible. Everything was very limited there—knowledge was limited—
so people were trying to do their best, trying to teach what they could.

CZ: Did you have things like classes in movement, voice, and singing?

KF: The program was two years; the morning was the basic stuff: movement and voice, and then usually a dance class of some form. Then the
afternoon would be an acting class, or theater history, or music, which
was never my specialty. We had this opera singer. The head of the drama
course took me and another girl for remedial singing lessons, because we
used to burst into tears during singing class. [laughter]

We had lots of movement. That's the thing I was struck by when I did
The Maids, the first theater I'd done in the UK; I was amazed by how ex-
cited everyone was about the movement that we did, and I was thinking,
"For fuck's sake, this is basic; it's below basic."

CZ: What happened after you finished drama school?

KF: Immediately after drama school—because you always knew you
weren't going to get employed as an actor, and you had to be able to
do something else—I taught a lot, because I'd taught drama from
when I was at school. And I've always had quite a technical mind, so I
was a lighting tech and a stage manager. I did a lot of that, and while
doing that, acting in fringe work, which we call co-op theater, auditioning for theater, for jobs in New Zealand, but doing terrible auditions. And trying to audition for commercials, doing terrible commercial auditions!

The first and only commercial I ever got was directed by Gaelene
Preston—she's a New Zealand film director; she made something called
Ruby and Rata. It's ironic that that's the only commercial audition I succeeded at, because she's considered a good film director, a frontrunner. It's
common there for directors to make commercials, as it is the only way they
can make money; that's how Lee Tamahori [director of *Once Were Warriors,*
1994] started.

CZ: It seems, in some ways, the relationship between New Zealand and Australia is very much like the relationship between Canada and the United States. Because a lot of actors feel if they really want to be successful, they have to work in the States.

KF: Except it's not that straightforward. It's not as if Australia is the big brother, although you'd imagine it would be. Certainly, when I was growing up, the question was always, "When are you going to England?" England being "home" for many people in New Zealand.

Also, when you move to Australia, you see how different it is. Australia is such a vast continent—as opposed to New Zealand. Australia is much more confused about its identity. It's confusing, because I feel like I have so many different influences and come from so many different places.

CZ: Do you feel a difference between yourself and British people? If you do, in what ways?

KF: Yeah, I do. Here, in England, I see the world as being a lot smaller and accessible. There are possibilities, and your life isn't limited. You have a different sense of the quality of life as well.

For instance, I have a place in Sydney, on the beach, and when I go there, I live a life opposite to the life I live here in London, which is mainly about work and socializing and being very busy. Whereas, in Sydney, it's about getting up and going for a swim, and having a coffee, then another little swim, then maybe some juice! That is impossible here; you couldn't see that as a life.

I also don't find people are straight with you here. People are very self-concerned. It's funny, I asked a good friend of mine, who's English, to do a reading with me of something that I'm interested in doing, just to hear it aloud rather than always reading the written words. She said,"Oh, no, I couldn't do it justice." I said,"That's not the point. It's nothing to do with you, I'm asking you a favor because you're my friend." But she thought there was more behind it. Whereas, when I've done the same thing in New Zealand, with my friends, they say, "Sure, we'll just have a cup of tea and we'll read it aloud."

Although, on the other had, the main reason that I'm here is that actors are better treated, certainly than in Australia. I feel I'm part of something here; I feel justified. I'm sure of what I'm doing, whereas, in

Australia, I don't really feel part of anything; I don't feel part of the film industry. And I don't know why that is. I've done a couple of films there—it's sort of weird. Here, I know the investors, I know the distributors, I know the people in business as well as the people who are making the films. And there, I don't know those people at all.

CZ: When did An Angel at My Table *(1990) come in the chronology of all of this, and how did you get that part?*

KF: It must have been in my second year out of drama school. Our year runs from January to December, not like the Northern hemisphere. Then I did a year of . . . I don't know what I was doing [laughs]. All that stuff, you know, operating lights for a women's comedy cooperative while they had major discussions about whether they'd call themselves a collaborative or a cooperative! And auditioning. I had been doing bad theater auditions, not doing myself justice, so when I got the audition script for *An Angel at My Table*, I thought, "If I don't do this well, then I'm wasting my time, I'm fooling myself, I have to stop acting."

CZ: It must have been a really big coup for you, to get the part in An Angel at My Table, *because Jane Campion had become known by that time for* Sweetie *(1989).*

KF: When I met Jane, no one had seen *Sweetie*. I knew nothing of film at all, I was completely film-illiterate, although I knew about Janet Frame, and I really liked the script. I thought it was the most amazing thing I'd ever read in my life, and I just knew that I could do it. Also, I knew that if I didn't do it well, it would be a terrible thing.

CZ: Did Jane Campion film chronologically, so that you could see what the two other girls who played you as a child were doing?

KF: No. We had a month's rehearsal, which is when I watched the girls acting. That was when it came to me that if I wasn't really precise, and good and truthful, I'd be fucked, because they were so much better than I was. And they had certain tiny little mannerisms that I knew Jane wouldn't ditch, that I had to do.

CZ: How strictly was the part scripted?

KF: Jane cut a lot before we shot it. I seem to remember sticking to the script, because it was such a magnificent piece of work, beautiful. Laura Jones writes the most incredible scripts.

CZ: I've heard that Jane Campion asks for a lot of input from her actors and works very closely with them. Did she allow for you to bring your own ideas to the role? Was the look of the character taken factually from the way that Janet Frame looked?

KF: Well, I had to eat a lot; they were always stuffing me with cakes and biscuits, until we ran out of money in Spain, and then we were all starving. They had these wigs made; it's compromise and trial and error when you're trying to get this part to work, particularly of a real person. And we had a really good makeup artist who helped with the age transformation, and the teeth, of course, which were made.

But as far as my relationship with Jane, we just spent a lot of time together. And in the rehearsal room, Jane would expect me to behave like Janet, which I found really difficult and fought against. I had to be myself to ask questions, to create a character to act. I suppose, more and more, they become the same thing—there's less definition between yourself and the character. Looking back now, you have a feeling as you would with anything of that scale, or when you're trying to be that true. You just have to trust the person, and I feel like I gave everything to Jane and trusted that she'd use it carefully.

CZ: Would you discuss issues like the diagnosis of schizophrenia and the treatment given to Janet in the institution?

KF: Oh yeah, all of that and what it meant. And also the actual autobiography itself was a great piece of resource material. Certainly the time, the era, what it was like, and the character's loneliness and shyness and fear.

There was a conflict in me, because I met Janet Frame and realized that we weren't actually doing a portrayal of Janet; we were doing a representation of Laura's script, which was based on Janet's autobiography, so it was always simply a representation, an interpretation of the material. For me, after I met Janet—Janet's very witty and very sharp and very smart— I thought, "I can never be that. I'm not as witty, and I'm not as intelligent as she is, and so I can't be that. I can only be as much as I am, added to the script." So, it's a different version of her from her real self. I would always ask myself, "If I was this character in this situation, what would I do?" and that was always the question, if I was lost. "If I was this person who was shy, fragile, and nervous, and had these physical characteristics, if I was in this situation in this country with these people, what would I do?" So it's a mixture of yourself and being that character. In a sense, it's your own response, altered by the situation and the personality you've got. And then there were things in myself that I felt, came from within me: scenes in the mental institute, the writing of the poetry, and the trying on of the father's boots. I remember Jane often trying to get me to do more. I could have all the truth of thought or emotion, whatever you want to call it, going through me, but I couldn't always express it cinematically enough, in a filmable way. So she was always trying to get me to do something, to have action in what I was doing. To somehow let it out, rather than keep it inside, which is a conflict in the character as well, because she kept so much inside.

CZ: Was that film a life-changing event for you?

KF: I think it was certainly life-changing because of the fact that it opened doors for me that I would never have known existed, but it hasn't made me into a "star" or pushed me in that direction. It meant that I left New Zealand, that I could work over here, that I have worked with really amazing people who have had a belief in my skills as an actor. I haven't had to prove myself, so it's been really luck. It's given me the basis of what I believe is good work, and valuable work, and that's something that I get the most satisfaction out of.

CZ: Do you use rushes when you film?

KF: Yeah, I always watch rushes. Always. Only because I don't like to do the same thing twice. Sometimes you think you're presenting something, and you realize, in fact, you're not at all, and often you think on the day you're shooting, "Oh, that was really good, that was really fucking hot." And then you realize it's this big nothing. I suppose I always use rushes in a positive way, in a constructive way, to see what's good, what needs to be broadened, and to make sure that the character has a lot of range, and not to repeat myself. If the character has certain aspects that I feel need to be revealed during the film, then I have to check that they're actually showing up on camera. I think you don't really have any judgment in the moment.

CZ: You've done quite a few films by now. Is there anything that's evolved in terms of your relationship to the camera?

KF: I know now that I love the camera. I felt before that I wasn't able to say that. *An Angel at My Table* was my first experience of being in front of a camera—I had no idea. But now I know that I love it. Also now, even though I looked through the camera lens all the time when I was shooting that film, I didn't know what I was doing. But now I look at an empty frame, the set-up, and from that, I use an image of how my physicality will fill it, to make it into a photograph that has dimension. And I often find that's a real clue: If I see the set-up, and the director's intentions with the set-up, then I know what they're thinking and I can fill that requirement.

CZ: Have you learned to use your face differently than when you first started? Is that what you mean by physicality? Are you talking about gestures and actions?

KF: I suppose if I see a frame, then I imagine what it requires to make it whole, into a piece of work, and that's my role.

CZ: But doesn't that make you self-conscious?

KF: Well, I don't know. Another thing that drama school taught us is that the more walls you have, the more restrictions, the freer you can be. If you have a solid base, then you can be as free as you like; you can't say, "My character wouldn't do this." You can do anything, and you've got to make it as interesting and as satisfying as possible.

CZ: But it's still got to be within the framework of what would be true to that character.

KF: But anything could be truthful. That's the weird thing. People are capable of so much, you know. Whatever you do *is* that character. It is.

CZ: Hasn't there got to be some sort of consistency? A character has certain restrictions on her behavior, personal desires, dislikes, and so on. There have to be some kind of parameters for the way a character would behave.

KF: Yeah, but those parameters are already set up. You don't have to establish them; they're set up in the script. You have many choices, and there's no right or wrong, and many of them could be truthful. And you've got to try to exploit as many of those choices as possible, so you don't get trapped by social conventions. Yeah, you do have to have a sense of the kind of personality, or an image of a character, but from there, I think it just works to make you more free, ideally. And you want the character to be changing, to not always be the same, to respond differently to every single moment in the film.

CZ: Do you find a difference in the way that female and male directors work on the set?

KF: Not if they're good. But, I think it's probably easier for bad male directors to work than it is for bad female directors.

CZ: I remember one woman I spoke with saying that you could tell woman directors when you had your period, and you had cramps . . .

KF: When I was doing *Shallow Grave* (1994) with Danny Boyle, it was really tense—there's the big fight at the end. We shot that at the end of the movie, and we were running out of film stock, because they'd made a slight mistake about the number of zeros in the amount of film stock ordered, so it was very, very tense. Also, I find, whenever I'm doing violent work, that I get irrationally angry—totally, irrationally upset and angry. I know it's a trait in me that I have to just ride with and not be carried away by it. We three actors [Ewan McGregor and Christopher Eccleston] were actually being very careful of each other and really chilling out. So when we were shooting, we were like [makes snarling noise], but whenever anyone called, "Cut," we'd all stop, lie back, hang loose, just try and stay calm. But it was incredibly tense because we thought we might not be able to finish the movie, the bond man was down their necks, they were running out of film stock, and we had this huge scene to do. And we had this prosthetic; I knew if I fucked it up the first time, it would take a two-hour change. It was really weird; we did the scene where I stab Chris, and Danny kept the take going, and I was on the floor hyperventilating, and everyone called, "Cut." And everyone rushed to Chris, because he was the one who had the prosthetic, saying, "Wow, that was amazing," and only the makeup artist came to me, because it seemed like I was going to faint. It was the weirdest thing, because I instantly got my period; it was like [noise of fluid escaping under pressure], because there was all this blood everywhere; I'd been soaking in it. And then we did another set-up, and I said to Danny, "It's weird; I got my period during that take." It's a terrible shock, stabbing someone with a knife; my heart leapt, it was horrific. But I was able to say that to Danny.

When I was working with Gillian Armstrong [*The Last Days of Chez Nous,* 1993], I had a really bad day, I was really tense, and I didn't want to do something because I was feeling off, and I had my period, and I found it almost impossible to say that to Gillian. It had something to do with one of the naked shots. I didn't want to run around with no clothes on top of this balcony, because I felt slobby and revolting. By the time I'd told her that, I felt really stupid for saying it. So it was a complete reversal of what you'd expect, really.

For me, there are certain qualities that I am inspired by in directors, and they occur in individuals, whether they're male or female. I think there's a certain childlike quality, and an ego that is amazing because it is totally sure of what it wants. Yet it's not self-protective in any way, but really strong and tough. I think directors are like perverts; they can be very perverse. And they love people, could lick them up, could eat them with their enthusiasm, and that's what inspires me. Along with intelligence and energy, and that happens whether people are male or female.

CZ: Could we talk about The Last Days of Chez Nous? *How did Gillian Armstrong work on the relationships of the people in the house?*

KF: I find it hard to talk about that because I don't want to be disloyal to Gillian or deny her anything. For me, Gillian is one of the those people who casts well, and then shoots what the actors do.

CZ: Do you feel like she left you alone and didn't give you a lot of direction?

KF: Yeah. And also at the time I felt it was Lisa's [Harrow's] film, so I just backed off. I didn't want to behave like I normally do. And Lisa's very, very dominant, and so for me to be myself—which is pretty dominant— would have been a real clash.

CZ: I found the relationships among the people in the film very complex; there's a lot of ambiguity about what's going on, which is interesting. That's why I asked how Gillian worked on the dynamic of the relationships amongst the people sharing the house, and the different couplings and uncouplings that happen in the course of the film.

KF: I think it was such a clash of personalities, that film. And that's what I mean when I say that Gillian casts really well. Bruno Ganz didn't know what he was getting himself into. Apparently, he read one of Helen Gardner's short stories on the plane on the way out, one about a woman who'd left a tampon in for too long, and extracted this green thing, and Bruno was just beside himself thinking, "What have I done, what am I doing, what am I letting myself in for!" [laughs] I got on really well with him, really well. He just got sick of being treated like a child, and actors often end up being treated like children.

CZ: Do you mean by Gillian?

KF: Just by the nature of the business. You're being told what to do twelve hours a day, and it can be deeply frustrating.

CZ: I thought it also interesting that the film had something that would be called "private moments" at The Actors Studio. It's an exercise where you do something that you would never do if anyone else were in the room, and it's meant to liberate you; it's given to actors who have trouble with what Stanislavski called being "private in public," letting their feelings or private behaviors be seen by an audience.

KF: Things that you personally would never do?

CZ: Yes, if I were leaping around the house dancing and singing, I would never do that if someone else was in the room, and the minute someone comes into the room, I would stop. That's a private moment. I felt like there were a lot of scenes like that in The Last Days of Chez Nous, *especially the scenes involving you. Like those scenes where you're dancing on the balcony.*

KF: I can understand the value of the exercise you're talking about, but I've become less and less interested in solo moments that I see as narcissistic—actors looking in the mirror at themselves.

CZ: But it's like those crazy dances that you do with Bruno; they're very uninhibited.

KF: Those are part of my normal life. For instance, I've been trying to kill someone every night for the last five months in *The Maids*. It started to drive me completely fucking insane, so we went out dancing in Liverpool. It was all set up that we'd go dancing, and we were all really excited about it. And Niamh [Cusack] had never gone to a club before in her life, which was shock horror for me: "Someone who has never been to a club?" I don't go very often, but when I do, it's really important, and I *have* to dance. So I just had to go for it, I *had* to let it rip. I have to let it out!

CZ: So Bruno Ganz didn't mind doing this sort of crazy dancing?

KF: It took him a while to get into it, but then he was really encouraging. It was like when he put the colander on his head in the film.

CZ: What did you think about the ending of the film? You're having an affair with your sister's husband, and you don't look happy, and Bruno gives you a look as only he can, that says, "This isn't working, I really screwed this up." I liked the ambiguity of it.

KF: But that's all Gillian. I asked Gillian, "Can't we have some hope? Why can't there be hope in this?" and she said, "No."

CZ: When you do a role like that, you know certain things about your character: you're pregnant, you've been abroad, you are very distant from your parents, you've been parented by your sister. Do you fill in the other parts for yourself mentally or imaginatively? Because your character has certain actions or behaves in ways that obviously have some meaning below the surface. For example, the first thing we see your character do is walk into the house after she's been away and rip away a huge chunk of cake that has been carefully baked and trimmed by her sister.

KF: I think it's a mix of things. It comes back to what I was saying before; it's to do with seeing the frame. I think, in that case, I saw the frame of where the cake was, and so you have to make a statement about the perfect piece of cake. It had to be all [makes slooshing, grabbing noises]; it had to be this big thing.

I think that where the actor and director meet is in the lens. I know that I saw the image of where the cake was, and remember knowing that it had to be this huge hand, and then, of course, regretting it, because I had to eat thirty-two pieces of cake the following day, to do the scene. Why didn't I take a smaller piece?

CZ: Have you had a really big battle of personalities with somebody on a set? How do you resolve things like that?

KF: I don't know, I think they damage me really badly. When I have been in difficult films or films where I feel my nature's been squashed, it's been devastating to me. I've not been able to act for six months after, so it has been really terrible, and shocking. But now I've just got to say, "I don't want to do that; I'm not going to put myself in that situation now."

CZ: But how could you determine in advance what the situation would be like?

KF: You really can't. Every film that I've done, I've done because I've believed in it, and because I felt strongly about the ideas that were being expressed, and that it was different, and adventurous, and exposing. And when I've come up against a director—it's not actors I've had problems with—who tries to limit me or tries to stop me from acting—that's the way I see it—it's really crushing. It's always been different, I've always dealt with it in different ways. I know that it will probably happen again, but I hope that it won't.

It's funny, *Shallow Grave* was great for me because I'd worked with Danny before, and I think he's an amazing man. But just before I did that, I'd done a real dog of a movie which was a really interesting and intriguing script, and I really trusted the people I was working with, but it turned out that it was never followed through. So when I had the opportunity to work with Danny, I said "I can't do this, I don't want to act." I'd been with Danny for half an hour—we were in the pub—and I agreed to do the film. And so I came out of *Shallow Grave* on top of the world, sure of what I was doing, knowing my role, that I support people, that I provide a base for people, that I provide strength for people to work from.

CZ: You're still at an early stage in your career, but do you sense any arc in your work since you began working in film?

KF: I know that I rely on other people, that I can't do it by myself; you need the support and the inspiration of other people. When I don't have that, I feel really lost. If I don't work six months or a year, that also really makes me feel lost. But when I do have that bond with other people, I know that I can rely on them for life, and I know that I have more people now than I had five years ago or ten years ago, and so it gives me a greater sense of security in what I'm doing.

When I look back on what I've done, all I know is that I've been exceptionally lucky, and I don't know why that is. Maybe there's nothing more to it than that. I would have ditched it long ago if I hadn't had that luck.

Career Highlights

Film: *An Angel at My Table* 90. *The Last Days of Chez Nous* 93. *Country Life* 94. *Shallow Grave* 94. *The Hanging Garden* (GENIEN) 97. *Welcome to Sarajevo* 97. *The Sound of One Hand Clapping* 98. *The Wisdom of Crocodiles* 98. *The Darkest Light* 99. *Fanny and Elvis* 99. *Intimacy* 2000. *The Point Men* 2001.

Theater: *The Maids* 97. *I Am Yours* 98. *In Flames* 2000.

Television: "Mr. Wroe's Virgins" 93. *A Village Affair* 94. *The Affair* 95. *Saigon Baby* 95.

Helen Mirren

[Acting] is placing yourself within the kaleidoscope of human
character, seeing yourself as clearly as you can within a part of
that, and then using the different elements within that scope .
. . it's not looking at yourself egotistically, but looking at your-
self as a human being, and what being a human being means.

CAROLE ZUCKER: *What was your background like? Where did you grow up,*
and what was the cultural climate like when you were growing up?

HELEN MIRREN: The fifties to sixties, basically, was my growing-up period.
I came from an upper-working class, lower-middle class background.
When I was younger, my father was a taxi driver, and then joined the civil
service in Britain, but on a very low level. He was born in Russia. He had
had a very good education, so although I was living in a working-class environment, my father was educated, and my mother was very bright. In
terms of a cultural environment, we had no money, so we didn't have TV,
we didn't go to the theater, and we didn't go to the cinema. There was very
little exposure to those sorts of things. If we went anywhere, we would go
very, very occasionally to the theater, but I don't really remember my parents even going to the theater until I was about thirteen or fourteen.

CZ: *What made you want to become an actor, if you weren't exposed to the*
theater or cinema?

HM: Well, my school had quite a good drama department. I went to a
Catholic convent school; not that my parents were Catholic, my parents
were sort of left-wing socialists.

CZ: Why did they send you to a convent school?

HM: Because it was the best school in the area that you didn't have to pay to go to. It was a parochial school, but it was part of the state-run school system, so it was free. It was very much a sort of Catholic young ladies' education, so they had drama, but it was only to develop your skills as a good housewife-and-mother kind of thing. The idea that you might actually use it as a profession was absolutely anathema to them; there was certainly no encouragement in that direction. They had a drama teacher who was really an elocution teacher to teach you to talk nicely; she was very bright, and she would have drama competitions and things. It was at school, when I got exposed to Shakespeare for the first time, that I really got interested.

CZ: Did your parents encourage you in that direction?

HM: Well, yeah. Of course, any parent likes you to do well at school, and do things at school that you're successful in. But certainly, subsequently, they didn't want me to be a professional actress, no. They were afraid I wouldn't succeed.

CZ: Then you went to teacher's college?

HM: Yeah. That was because I couldn't go to drama school, because my parents would never have let me go. Not that at that point they could have had much say, but there was no economic basis for me to go to drama school at all, so I had to go somewhere I could get a grant, a scholarship, and that was for teacher's training. But I chose a teacher's training college that did drama.

CZ: And that was the New College of Speech and Drama? How did you feel about going there?

HM: It was okay. I mean, it was exciting to be in London and away from home. It was the first step out of the home environment, and living on my own, and so forth, so all of that was great.

CZ: And then you joined The National Youth Theatre.

HM: Yes, at the same time, more or less, when I was finishing school and beginning college, I joined The National Youth Theatre, and that was really what was most helpful or productive in terms of me becoming a professional actress.

CZ: Did they have formal classes?

HM: No, they just did productions in the school holidays.

CZ: Was there any emphasis on how one could develop a character?

HM: No, not at all. It was just moving large numbers of kids around the stage and doing Shakespeare. They would always do the Shakespeare plays that required a lot of boys to run on and off the stage, like *Julius Caesar* and *Coriolanus*, plays like that.

CZ: Did you have any ambitions when you were with The National Youth Theatre, about becoming a star, a great lady of the theater, that sort of thing? Do you consider yourself to be an ambitious person in general?

HM: I didn't used to think of myself as being ambitious, but I think subsequently I've come to realize that I probably was ambitious in my own way. I wasn't ambitious for the obvious things. But when you say "great lady of the theater," yes, I was ambitious for that, definitely.

CZ: And did you have any role models for that sort of ambition?

HM: Yes, in the sense of the respect and the roles, I was quite influenced by what I'd read about the Sarah Bernhardts and the Eleanora Duses of the world. I wasn't so influenced by modern movie stars or even theater stars, but I loved the idea of these great divas of the stage.

CZ: I've read that the people you wanted to emulate were Anna Magnani and Monica Vitti, who would be quite different from Duse or Bernhardt.

HM: Well, certainly in terms of acting, that's true. I didn't admire Monica Vitti for her acting, just the way she looked, and the way she was in those wonderful Italian movies like *L'Avventura* (1960). I think that was the first foreign film I ever saw, and I was blown away by it. Just to be Italian, to be Monica Vitti and walk around in nice clothes on an Italian island would be great. But Anna Magnani, totally, in terms of being an actress, she was the only one. You can never hope to emulate anyone, there's no point, but you can learn from them.

CZ: What do you think it was about Magnani that attracted you?

HM: Her liveliness on screen. And I'm only talking about seeing her on screen; I never saw her on stage, although she did a lot of stage work. Just her liveliness, and her presence. I don't mean that in terms of her being a big presence, but the fact that she is so present in the moment, and so utterly real.

CZ: When you began acting, it seems that you became almost immediately successful very early on, when you were about nineteen, and then did a lot of the major roles in classical theater when you were in your twenties. What kind of a time was that for you emotionally, to be so young and to become famous so quickly?

HM: Well, you're not really aware of the fame side of it, and it was fame within a fairly esoteric circle. But yes, I was successful very, very quickly; almost as soon as I entered the profession I became successful, and stayed successful in a sense. But at that time, I was more obsessed with achieving what I wanted to achieve, which was the respect of my peers and recognition as a great classical actress. Although I was getting great reviews and a lot of exposure, there's a long way off between getting some good reviews and being recognized as a great actress. And Shakespeare's very hard. It's like training to be an opera singer; it's very, very difficult, and you're constantly confronted by your own inadequacies.

CZ: Did you ever feel when you were acting with people who had been to traditional drama schools that you might have benefitted from a classical training?

HM: No, it didn't make any difference. I was in exactly the same place as they were. I think the whole sense of drama training is a fantasy anyway. I think the only training you can have in reality, is doing it. In Shakespeare, it's to develop the vocal skills, which you can't possibly learn at drama school; you can only learn that by having to go on stage every night and do it.

CZ: You played Cleopatra in Antony and Cleopatra *when you were just starting as an actor, and then again in your late thirties. Did you think when you were doing it the second time, about the ways you had developed as an actor?*

HM: Yes, of course. And I hope I'll do it again. Absolutely. [Mirren played Cleopatra again in 1998 at the National Theatre.]

CZ: What conclusions or observations did you have about the experience? What were the differences you noticed?

HM: I knew the lines; that was a great advantage. Going into rehearsal, I found that I knew the part, which was great. It means you can go on from there; you don't have to struggle around learning the lines for the first three or four weeks. I mean, every Shakespearean role should be assayed at least twice. Anyone who does Shakespeare understands that. You need at least two goes at a role to get anywhere close to what your potential in the role is, and with a role like Cleopatra, I don't think two goes is enough, you probably need at least three goes.

CZ: *Is there anything that you want to do now in the Shakespearean canon?*

HM: No. The trouble is there are not enough great roles for women in Shakespeare. He wrote some great roles, but not enough of them. I have played all of them. Not to say I shouldn't want to play them again. The truth is Lady Macbeth is not a very good role; it's not as good a role as Macbeth. So there are not that many roles, unfortunately.

CZ: *There was a certain point in the eighties when you seemed to have turned from the stage to film; you did very little stage work after that. Was there a reason behind that decision?*

HM: Well, because I'd spent a lot of time working on the stage, learning my craft, I suddenly realized there was a whole arena of work that I was completely unknowledgeable about. So I had reached a certain level of accomplishment—I don't mean success—in the theater, because my personal understanding of success was always to do with how accomplished I was, and not how "successful" I was. I'd reached a level of accomplishment, but, as I say, I was a child; I knew nothing about film. I'd done a couple of movies, but I had been completely at sea, not knowing what the hell I was doing, and I just thought it was time to learn. So I deliberately stepped away from the theater. All that time I was in the theater, I was regularly offered film roles. But I'd turned them down because I was already committed to doing *Hamlet* or yet another season with The Royal Shakespeare Company, and I couldn't walk away from it. Not that I wanted to, incidentally. That was what I wanted to do. I had managed to squeeze in a couple of film roles, but as I say, I knew nothing about it, and I thought it was time to get a little knowledge going.

CZ: How did you feel when you first saw yourself on screen?

HM: Oh, horrified. I'm still fairly horrified; I don't like to watch myself very much.

CZ: Do you go back and see your films? I know some people won't do that at all.

HM: It's not that I won't, but I can't be bothered. I literally just can't be bothered. There's a lot of work that I've just never seen.

CZ: Do you ever use rushes as a tool?

HM: I do a bit, yes, I make myself go to rushes. Not a lot, usually just in the initial stages of a film. But, in general, no.

CZ: What's the big difference for you between acting for the stage and for the film?

HM: Money.

CZ: Money! [laughs] That's it?

HM: Money and hours. That really is the big difference. The hours are so different, and the social life is very different. Otherwise, really, the job is the same. Although you obviously use completely different surface techniques, the interior work, the real work, is exactly the same.

CZ: Can you talk about some of those surface techniques?

HM: You don't talk so loudly for the movies, and you only use the bit of your body that's in the shot, whereas on stage, you're using all of your body, all the time.

CZ: What do you think makes great film acting? Or what do you consider a great performance?

HM: Liveliness. Aliveness.

CZ: And who has that in your opinion?

HM: Well, Anna Magnani. And you know who had it in bucketloads— Louise Brooks. I would say look to Louise Brooks for inspiration. Otherwise, I always look at children and animals. And the younger the children are, the better—babies, not like awful six-year-old, trained theatrical children. Babies and animals, especially animals, are brilliant film actors because they're totally present in the moment. They're alive; they're completely unselfconscious. But, of course, you can't be like that, because you have to hit your mark, and you have to know what the next line is, and who the actor is you work with, so you can't be an animal, or animal-like. But you can learn from animals.

CZ: What makes you take a role? Do you feel you need to have empathy with the values and emotions of your character? Is there any sort of role that you won't do?

HM: Many roles I won't do, many roles. Empathy, I'm not sure. You have to have an understanding of the character. Not necessarily an empathy, but an understanding, a deep understanding, even if it's in an area of yourself that you don't like to look into too often. But you don't necessarily have to have an empathy with the character, no.

CZ: When you say that there are things that you won't do, I remember seeing an interview you did in the "Hollywood Women" series, made for British television, and you said that Pretty Woman *(1990) was "disgustingly immoral." Is that the sort of role that you're talking about, when you say there are parts you would never play?*

HM: Oh, listen, if I'd been at a certain age, and someone had asked me to play that role, I'm sure I would have done it. But maybe I would have had the moral rectitude to turn it down. The trouble with movies is that you never really know the film that's going to come out. I know that the original story of that particular film was a much darker, more serious, more truthful story about what it's like to be a young hooker on Hollywood Boulevard, instead of that appalling romantic fantasy trash. It's bad enough that girls come to Hollywood hoping for something and become hookers anyway, but to romanticize it was horrible.

CZ: Was there ever a part that you had a lot of difficulty in understanding? Do you ask for help? Do you find directors helpful in that sense?

HM: No, no. You can never ask a director for help in that area, I don't think. Not in understanding character, because they're always going to be talking from their own perspective. It's often a man, but even if it's not a man, and it's a woman, they'll be talking from their own understanding of their own life. You have to approach a character from an understanding of your life, your realities.

CZ: So you've generally not found directors very helpful in discussing character. Was there ever a time when you just said, "I can't crack this person; I can't figure out why they do what they do?"

HM: Yes, often. The best thing is not to think about it, quite honestly, and just carry on regardless. You do in real life. We don't all know why we do everything all the time. In fact, eighty-five percent of the time, you do things that if someone said to you afterwards, "Why did you do that?", you'd have absolutely no idea why you did it. So I don't feel the necessity to explain everything, to have an explanation for everything that a person or a character does. The best thing is just to do it, and not think.

CZ: What's your idea of an ideal actor–director relationship?

HM: My favorite director is a New Zealand director called Geoff Murphy. He has only four directions, and they always start with "That was fantastic." Whatever you've done, it was fantastic, and then he always says, "It's fantastic, only let's do one more, and give me a little bit more," or "That was fantastic; let's do one more, only give me a little bit less," or "That was fantastic; let's do one more, a bit faster or slower." And honestly, that covers every single direction you can possibly need. And combinations: faster and more, or faster and less, slower and more . . . that really is everything you need from a director. Sometimes, it's nice if they give you a little tip like, "Why don't you play with your hair in that shot, or fiddle with something," or "Why don't you try and take your hat off slowly?" Sometimes they come up with a nice idea like that, which is the most helpful of all.

CZ: Are you an actor who likes rehearsal?

HM: I like rehearsal in the theater; I don't much like rehearsal for film. Although it's necessary, I'm always frightened of rehearsing for film, because I'm frightened I'm going to do it brilliantly, and then never be able to do it again that way.

CZ: How much do you rely on instinct on the spot when you're performing?

Can you remember any moment that was completely unplanned, but which turned out to be something like an epiphany or a happy accident in either theater or film?

HM: It happens more often in theater, because, obviously, you're freer, you're more in control of your circumstances in the theater. And in the theater, I try and make it happen every night. Film work is a far more controlled environment, so it has less chance of happening in film. But it's what you work for; it's what you work towards.

CZ: You talked in one interview, quite astutely, about the idea of instinct and technique, and going through the long process of learning technique to differentiate a good accident from a bad accident.

HM: Well, that comes from Francis Bacon, who's always been my great inspiration as far as acting is concerned. Francis Bacon, who talked about that in terms of painting. I felt it, because I'd been through a similar process of learning my technique while learning how to do Shakespeare. And the same is true in movies: You have to learn the technique in order to be able to throw it away. You can't throw the technique away before you learn it.

CZ: Do you find that you're frustrated in films? Do you ever feel that you don't have the same freedom you have on stage?

HM: No, no, it's just that everything in film is more concentrated. It's concentrated into a moment, into a second, and it's very addictive like that, it's very hyper. It's exhausting.

CZ: You said at one point that your original ambition was to be a female Alec Guinness, and to take on different personalities, and constantly change your appearance. Later you said that acting comes from revealing what's within you, and not in assuming disguises. When I look at the roles that you've played, you do seem very different from part to part. I guess the other half of that question is, "How do you make a role personal for yourself?" Do you use imagery, memories, what they would call, in Stanislavskian terms, "affective memory"?

HM: If the characters I play come out very differently, it's nothing to do with things that I'm putting on the personality from the outside. It's all to do with looking at a different aspect of yourself. It's not a constant searching of your own navel, either. It's placing yourself within the kaleidoscope of human character, seeing yourself as clearly as you can within a part of that, and then using the different elements within that scope. In other words, it's not an ego thing, it's not looking at yourself egotistically, but looking at yourself as a human being, and what being a human being means.

CZ: Do you ever feel that you've learned something about your own life from the characters that you've played? Or that things going on in your own life can correspond to a part you've chosen?

HM: I think I've found out about myself through playing certain roles. Or, at least, I've found out not about myself, but more about humanity, through playing certain roles. And the better the writing is, obviously the more you find out. If the work is by Shakespeare or Chekhov, you find out a great deal. There's always something to be thought about, considered. But I don't take my roles personally at all. I don't see them as a personal diary of my development.

CZ: Can we talk about your preparation for one role in detail? For example, how has your work on the character of Jane Tennison, in Prime Suspect, *evolved?*

HM: I honestly don't work on it at all. I didn't right from the beginning. I had no preparation time, because I was shooting another film. I had to leave the set at four o'clock in the afternoon and start shooting on Jane Tennison at six the next morning, having had absolutely no rehearsal whatsoever, not even a read-through.

I did a little bit of research. I did talk to some policewomen; I felt that was very necessary. But it was minimal. I just started it; I just went on from day to day, and I still do. I just look at the scene, think "What's it about?" and "Where should I stand?" and "I think it would be good if I did this here," and that's it. I honestly don't think about it for one second.

CZ: You don't see an evolution in terms of her relationships with men, her intimacy problems?

HM: Not really, no. Obviously, as time progressed, I was involved to a certain extent with the developments of the script, and we'd think "Well, maybe it's time for her to have an affair" or "It would be good if we did this." It has to do with what we think's a good idea, really. It's nothing to do with evolution of character, or psychology.

I don't tend to think psychologically, in general, when performing. I don't make psychological investigations. I don't in my real life, and I don't in my work life. I can't be bothered with all of that. It's what matters in the moment that matters to me. I'm of the Gerard Depardieu school of acting, which is, "You want me to play a gangster, I'll play a gangster. You want me to be a housekeeper, I'll play a housekeeper." You just do it, you don't think about it. It's better not to think too much.

CZ: What about your physical self? Certainly, watching you perform, it seems like one of the defining characteristics of your acting style is your comfort with your body. Do you work at that, and on relaxation and concentration? Do you find that you're ever self-conscious or vain? We can put that in the context of a particular film—The Cook, The Thief, His Wife & Her Lover *(1989), since it's so much about the body and bodily functions.*

HM: I thought *The Cook, The Thief* was a great piece of literature on the page. I was terrified of doing it because I didn't want to spend most of my day walking around without any clothes on. But it was a part of the movie and it had to be done, so I did it. If you're in a Peter Greenaway movie, you're in such a strange world anyway, it makes things it would appear impossible to do, possible. But in terms of concentration, relaxation, no, none of that. I mean, I think in terms of exercise, the best exercise for actors is yoga, because of what it does for your spine and your mind. Having said that, I don't practice yoga; I have done in the past, very briefly.

CZ: How was working with Greenaway different from working with directors up until that point, since he's so painterly?

HM: The truth is he's exactly the same as everybody else; it's just that the material is completely different. But the process of working is exactly the same as any film director. He makes it very comfortable for you; I loved working with him. Obviously, he has an immensely clear idea of the look that he wants. I'm very visual; I like the visual arts a great deal; I get a great deal of pleasure from it. If you feel you're in good hands, visually, I think that's one of the greatest gifts a director can give you. It's when I don't feel that I'm in good hands visually that I feel uncomfortable with directors. As long as I feel they have a strong visual style—and even moreso with Peter, it wasn't just that it was a strong visual style, it was a visual style that I loved. I thought it was remarkable and I couldn't wait to get to the set, because I wanted to be in that environment.

CZ: Did you feel that you had to understand what the film was about on an intellectual level?

HM: I had to understand what it was about for myself. It doesn't mean that what I thought it was about for myself had anything to do with what the film ultimately might have been about. But I had to understand why Georgina was where she was, why she was doing what she was doing. But, having said that, as I say, I very rarely think of things in psychological terms; I think of them more in general human terms, mythological terms.

CZ: Can you explain what that means? Georgina is in an abusive relation-ship with Michael Gambon's character, is obviously more refined than he is, has a suspect sexual past that is alluded to by Gambon, but other than that, we're given very little information about her, and that's true of a lot of your characters, I find.

HM: What I mean, is, instead of thinking, "Why is this person like this; what's the fuck-up?" you think, "This happens; women are in abusive relationships; this is the archetypal abusive relationship." So I'm doing this to expose the universality of that, rather than the specificity of it.

CZ: In The Mosquito Coast *(1986), the character of the mother in that is quite enigmatic. Why is she with her megalomaniac husband, even at the risk to her children? I think it's a good film, but I found your character really puzzling. Did you?*

HM: No, because I'd read the book. When it was made into a movie, there are huge lumps missing that would make the character understand-able. And because the lumps are missing, you don't understand the char-acter. But I understood the character. I didn't empathize with the charac-ter, but I understood her. She was much more of a partner in the book; they're in it together, so they're adventurers. She's a very creative person in the book, and a strong person. She leaves her husband, but then realizes she can't exist on her own out in the jungle, and has to go back. I argued for those things to be put into the film, but they weren't.

CZ: What happens when you have what they call in Hollywood "creative differences" with a director or with another actor? How do you solve those sort of problems?

HM: I don't really have them with other actors. I mean, I've worked with actors who are kind of "assholes," as they say, just difficult and hopeless. You give them a wide berth, basically, and let them get on with it. I have had creative differences with, not a lot of directors, only one really. As I've said, it was really to do with making the character stronger than she was.

CZ: How do you feel about the distinctions made between the "method" and classical acting, and this whole notion that "English actors act from the head, American actors act from the guts."

HM: I don't really know what that means any more. Everybody acts the same, as far as I can make out. We all learn our lines, and we all think we're shit, and we all worry about what we look like, and that's about it, really.

I think there is one real difference between English—let alone French, Italian, German actors—and American actors. You know, Europe is a big place—it's not just Britain—so let's say "European" actors: Polish, Russian, Hungarian. I think the thing that is remarkable about American actors, although it's both remarkable and it's their great downfall, is that they jump very easily into emotion, which is great. Their facility to reach into an emotional well and just jump headfirst in, and be unashamed and unafraid of doing that, is remarkable and admirable. However, the down side of that is that it is facile. It's facile emotion, it's not real, it's false. It's sort of a reproduction of an emotion. When you have emotional acting from European actors, it's far more real. But I hate to make judgments about actors and acting, because you're always wrong.

CZ: But, certainly someone like Marlon Brando could not be accused of using facile emotion.

HM: Brando is a huge, brilliant technician, is what Brando is. The greatest film technician.

CZ: I don't understand what you mean when you say that.

HM: He understands how to use the camera. He knows where to flick his eyes, he knows how to position his body, he knows what angle his face looks best at. He's a technician. It's very self-conscious. And what so-called method acting is, is in fact, a method of self-consciousness. It's not real life; people in real life are not like that. You go into the street, into the supermarket, anywhere, and see how real people are, they're not like that. That's why Anna Magnani is so great, you see, because Anna Magnani is real. So, if you saw someone like Harvey Keitel or Christopher Walken in a checkout, you'd think, "What is that wanker doing there, nosing around?" They wouldn't be real. I'm not saying I don't admire them, I do—Harvey Keitel actually is one of my favorite actors—but you mustn't confuse it; it is a very heightened technique, and it's very, very self-conscious.

CZ: I find your acting very real, and remarkably simple. In the work of a lot of actors there are usually startling, tour de force *moments in their performances. I can't say I find that in your work, because it all seems so natural to me.*

HM: I take that as a great compliment.

CZ: Something I find quite interesting about the British is that they don't want to make heroes out of their actors. That's what I seem to be hearing from you, as well—acting's a job, you just get up and do it. British actors seem to really go out of their way to show what regular blokes they are. It's very much in opposition to the Hollywood experience, where stardom is such a big thing.

HM: Well, a hero is one thing, a star is another. Are you saying British people don't want to make stars out of their actors? Or Americans want to make heroes out of their actors?

CZ: I feel that most British actors I've talked to aren't really concerned about being stars, whereas for many American actors, that is their goal. Not all of them, on either side.

HM: I think that's very, very true. There is a distastefulness about the star system in Britain. It's not to say that we don't enjoy stars, and love them, and think about them and obsess about them as much as the American public does, but I guess amongst the acting fraternity, yes, there is a distastefulness about that. You are supposed to undermine or underplay your own personality. I don't know why this is; I have no idea. It is true, though.

CZ: Do you have any feelings about people like Alan Rickman and Jeremy Irons who do big megabucks American movies, and play the villains. Some actors feel that they've sold out in some way.

HM: Well, I think that's just silly. I don't understand what *sold out* means, anyway. Sold out what? They're working actors like the rest of us, you know. You can just as easily betray your talent by playing some naff role in a rep in England, as you can playing a naff role in a big movie in America.

But I have to say I am irritated by the tendency in American movies to constantly cast the villain as a British person, which I think is a form of racism that's showing its head in Hollywood.

CZ: Why do you think it's racism? Aren't the British cast because they're able to bring a certain kind of panache—to "class up" a film?

HM: No, it's because it's the one group that you can happily cast as a villain and not be accused of racism, except by me. If you were constantly casting Blacks as the villain, or Jews or Germans or Latinos as the villain, you would be accused of racism. It seems you can constantly cast British people as the villain and get away with it. Well, not as far as I'm concerned. However, that is not to say Alan wasn't incredibly brilliant in that movie that he did where he was the villain—he was brilliant. Now, I have no problem with that.

CZ: There is a certain sense, I think, in which British actors can manage a kind of theatrical performance style that American actors, for the most part, can't or won't do. There are exceptions to that of course, like Al Pacino or Nicolas Cage, who can be highly theatrical. I can't think of someone who would have been able to do what Tim Roth did in Rob Roy. *I think it's the capability of bringing a certain outrageousness and technical prowess to the reading of dialogue that is the reason why they're hired, rather than out of any racism.*

HM: I disagree; I think there's a whole canon of American actors who can do that. Starting with Marlon, Al Pacino, and going down through many, many other actors who probably never get the chance. I think there are plenty of American actors who can do that.

CZ: The other difference that I see in American films is that women are overlooked once they're over forty; there are only a few who manage to hang on by their fingernails. Yet you're working constantly, now more than ever. You obviously must be happy about that, but how do you feel about that difference?

HM: It's devastating. Yes, I am working, it's great, but I don't have the choice that a man in my position would have, nowhere near the choice.

CZ: Was it a deliberate strategy or was it happenstance that you chose to work on smaller movies and independent features?

HM: I think it's a combination of happenstance and choice. I mean, obviously, the films have to get made, and they've got to be interested in you being in them for anything to happen at all. But I've always said I'd prefer to play a large role in a very low-budget film than a small role in a very big-budget film, and that is sort of the way I go. And if that's not available, I'll just go and work in the theater.

CZ: What happens to you when you feel like your creative juices aren't flowing? Does that ever happen? Do you ever improvise as a way of getting through a problem area?

HM: Oh yes, a lot. A lot.

CZ: What sort of improvisation would that be? Would it revolve around an emotional area you were dealing with in the scene? Do you find that other actors are responsive to doing that?

HM: Some are, some aren't. It's basically saying what is being said, but in different words, or speaking out the interior, the subtextual line, talking that out. I do it in Shakespeare as well.

CZ: The series Prime Suspect *must bring people closer to you in the sense of your being more well known. Do you feel that it gives you less of an opportunity to observe people unnoticed?*

HM: It probably does, but I'm not even aware of that. I'm usually blissfully unaware of the fact that I've been recognized. It seems to go over my head. Other people that I'm with notice it, but I'm always unaware of it. So I just kind of carry on regardless.

CZ: Is there anything that you've been able to identify as a problem area in your acting?

HM: That's been my life's work, doing that to myself. Constantly criticizing myself, and trying to be more of this and less of that. That is what it's all about, as far as I'm concerned. That is what I do on a daily basis when I'm working.

But having said that, I try not to think about what I'm doing too much. To not think is a very difficult thing, as anyone who's practiced meditation knows. To not think is the hardest thing of all. To empty your mind is a very, very difficult thing to do, and that is a very good state to achieve in acting—a sort of controlled emptiness of mind. "Don't think. Be."

Career Highlights

Film: *The Long Good Friday* 80. *Excalibur* 81. *Cal* (BAFTAN, Cannes) 84. *The Mosquito Coast* 86. *The Cook, The Thief, His Wife & Her Lover* 89. *The Madness of King George* (AAN, BAFTAN, Cannes) 94. *Some Mother's Son* 96. *Teaching Mrs. Tingle* 99. *Last Orders* 2001. *No Such Thing* 2001. *Gosford Park* 2001.

Theater: *All's Well That Ends Well* 67. *Troilus and Cressida* 68. *Much Ado About Nothing* 68–69. *Enemies* 70. *Hamlet* 70. *Miss Julie* 71. *Macbeth* 74. *The Seagull* 75. *Teeth 'n' Smiles* 75. *The Duchess of Malfi* 80–81. *The Faith Healer* 81. *Extremities* 84. *A Month in the Country* 97. *Antony and Cleopatra* 65, 83, 98. *Orpheus Descending* 2000.

Television: *Cousin Bette* 71. *As You Like It* 78. *Blue Remembered Hills* 79. *Cymbeline* 83. *Cause Célèbre* 87. *Losing Chase* (GG) 96. *Prime Suspect* (BAFTA [four-time winner]; Emmy for Best Actress) 90–present. *The Passion of Ayn Rand* (Emmy, GGN, SAGN) 99.

Roshan Seth

I try to be watchful, to be ruthlessly honest in discarding anything that is false, that is not coming from my "true voice" . . . . One cannot breathe naturally until the body is in relaxation. The voice will not be "true" and free until the breathing is natural. Breath carries feeling. Breath gives you life. Without it, you are a corpse.

CAROLE ZUCKER: Can you talk about your years growing up? You were raised in Patna, Bihar, in India. What was the cultural milieu like?

ROSHAN SETH: Patna, in Bihar, was and still is halfway between the sticks and a city, what is known as a *moufassil* (provincial) town. My cultural horizon as a child encompassed Hindus, Muslims, Sikhs, Jains, Buddhists, Christians, British, and a host of other ethnic, religious, and national communities. Yet I can't say it was a cosmopolitan horizon, because dominating it were a majority of Hindus, themselves a bewildering mosaic of castes and sub-castes and sub-sub-castes.

Within this broad cultural milieu, my parents were unusual. My mother got a teacher's training degree from London University and joined the Bihar government as Inspectress of Schools, and was later the principal of a women's college. My father, in comparison, was not a cultural freak. My father was educated in Lahore and at Cambridge in England. He came to Patna as a professor of biochemistry at the Patna Medical College. His first marriage ended tragically when his wife of six months died. He married, many, many years later, my mother, in 1941, when it was socially and culturally unacceptable for a Hindu to marry a Muslim.

Neither parent was orthodox in a religious sense; in fact, my father was an agnostic in the way that Buddhists are. My parents were rational, liberal, humanistic; there was a strong emphasis on the "perennial" philosophies, which are common to all religions. On my birth certificate, under the column marked religion, my father had entered—no doubt to the total astonishment of the establishment—"Religion of God." My father had a sense of humor when it came to things like that. My parents views were not uncommon within the educated classes—after all, similar views were being espoused by men like Gandhi and Nehru!

My grandmother, who lived with us when we were children, was a strong influence. She was a wonderful storyteller in a Dickensian sort of way, and a natural actor to boot: her mock tears could move us profoundly. My mother has all the makings of an actor but chose to confine her performances to her family and friends. It has taken me very nearly all my adult years to accept and feel comfortable with my cultural freakishness, and it has been the cause of much inner mental and emotional turmoil, particularly since the acting profession relies heavily on and reinforces stereotypical images in the minds of audiences.

CZ: What sort of school did you go to?

RS: I went to a Catholic missionary school in Patna to begin with, run by German nuns, and then a boys' boarding school when I was eleven. The Doon School is a secular fee-paying institution—expensive by Indian standards—modeled along the same lines as Eton and Harrow in England. It gave us an excellent, all-round education with a strong emphasis on the building of self-reliance, social confidence, and service to the country.

CZ: You've already answered this to a certain extent, but who would you say influenced you most while you were growing up?

RS: I was malleable and easily influenced—too easily. Especially by adults or teachers who appeared to show an interest in me. I was very susceptible to their kindness and patient understanding.

I was very influenced by the characters I saw in the cinema, particularly American Westerns produced in the forties and fifties. My heroes ranged from Jimmy Stewart and Gary Cooper to Ava Gardner and Rita Hayworth. I knew nothing about the lives of these actors; we didn't have movie magazines as children in Patna. It was their roles in the stories they filmed that influenced me, particularly the "goodness" of the hero and the frailty of the heroine always rescued from evil by the good guy. In my dreaming, I was the good guy loved by the good gal.

CZ: Were you involved in the arts as a child or adolescent? Did you go to the cinema, the theater, other art forms?

RS: As a child, no—other than the Sunday evening movie at the local school. As an adolescent, to a very limited extent in the annual school play or as an extracurricular activity. I do recall being very shy, introverted, almost awkward in the presence of grown-ups. The word *arts* or the idea of a future life in the arts formed no part of my vocabulary, nor any of my dreaming. They were as remote as the planets. What I did discover when I was at school was that sport cost me more effort than the enjoyment it brought, and acting in a play not only gave me greater pleasure for less effort, but made me feel good about myself.

CZ: Was there encouragement from your family or a teacher in your college to become an actor?

RS: No. Neither family nor teachers nor friends encouraged me to become an actor, though none stood in the way of my ever-increasing theatrical activities in my post-graduate years at university, and with several amateur groups in Delhi. Acting was simply not on anyone's list of good career choices for a young man with a good education. It was on *my* list, though, but I had to keep my secrets for fear that disclosure would doom them to failure.

CZ: You went to London to train at LAMDA in 1964. Can you discuss what the transition was like for you, to move from India to London?

RS: I went to London to audition at RADA, and wasn't given a place. So I went on to audition for The Bristol Old Vic School, LAMDA, and The Webber Douglas. I secured places at Bristol and LAMDA, with the latter offering me a bursary and a place in the special one-year advanced course designed specifically for young professional American actors who wished to expose themselves to a more classical training, especially of Shakespeare and Restoration Comedy.

The transition from Delhi to London was the fulfilment of a personal dream, albeit a private dream. I knew that a course of training was essential for a serious professional actor. I knew also that I simply had to get away from the small, narrow, almost asphyxiating confines of Indian middle-class aspiration. I wanted to grow up; I wanted to widen and deepen my experience of life. I wanted to be independent without people breathing down my neck, telling me what they thought was best for me, and I wanted above all to start living the life of an actor in a milieu where others were doing the same.

CZ: Can you talk about the orientation of LAMDA at the time? How did they teach you, for example, to work on characterization?

RS: LAMDA's orientation was similar to that at the Old Vic School—not the Bristol Old Vic. In a nutshell, one that tried to combine the best aspects of the British vocal tradition in performance with the best aspects of the European physical tradition. Michael MacOwan was the Principal and Norman Ayrton the Vice-Principal. Both had been associated with Michel St. Denis at the Old Vic School, and it was St. Denis who brought to England the European tradition. MacOwan was a director before turning to training. He and Ayrton were superb teachers. I had a soft spot for MacOwan, who was like a guru. I thought the approach to characterization, for instance, was through careful script analysis, followed by a finding-it-for-yourself-through-whatever-means, that produced the desired end results—it could be from without or from within, or based purely on imaginative will.

CZ: Did you harbor any ambitions at the time about becoming famous? Do you feel that you're an ambitious person?

RS: Oh, yes! Show me an actor that doesn't want to be considered great.

CZ: When you graduated, did you go the normal route of doing provincial rep? What sorts of places did you play in and what sorts of roles?

RS: More or less. I began in TV, then went to Crewe Rep. after about a year. That was followed by a season at the Flora Robson Playhouse in Newcastle-Upon-Tyne, and then the Gateway Theatre in Chester. I got what might be described as "oddball" roles—mainly character parts. I played a lot of doddery and dithering old men, much to the amusement of my colleagues, and much to my own growing frustration.

CZ: Among your credits is the RSC world tour of Peter Brook's production of A Midsummer Night's Dream. *As far as I know, he did two productions, one with Judi Dench and Ian Richardson, and another, which I saw in New York, which was a circus-themed version with a marvelous all-white set with trapezes. Which were you involved in, and what part did you play? What was it like to work with Peter Brook?*

RS: I was in the production of *The Dream* that you saw in New York. About seventy percent of the company in that production were recast for a world tour in '72–'73. I was part of the fresh cast chosen by Peter Brook after extensive auditions with him in England. I was one of four fairies, and I understudied Puck. Working with Peter Brook was another dream come true for me.

I had seen the production you saw when it played the Aldwych Theatre and never before had I seen, in the theater, anything so lively, joyous, and wonderful. Not everyone in the company took to Peter Brook. He is taciturn, demanding, and unforgiving—not unlike an Indian guru. The trick is to surrender yourself and your mind to men like Brook. I adored him and still do. Peter Brook shunned everything that appeared to him to be imitative, dead, unthought, false. He accepted everything that appeared to him life-affirming. He is an excellent teacher, too.

CZ: You seem to have worked quite frequently for both the RSC and for the National Theatre. Can you discuss what ultimately made you leave England and return to India? You talk in one interview about being afraid of losing your "Indianness." Is that what you felt happening to you? Did you feel that you would have more opportunities to play different sorts of roles in your own country?

RS: Had Brook invited me to join his International Company in Paris, I would not have hesitated for a single moment. I think Brook knew that I did not possess the mental and physical equipment necessary for the kind of work he was doing at the time. So after the *Dream* tour ended, I found myself in a kind of colorless limbo in London doing rather indifferent work to keep body and soul together. I was also very distracted by a love affair that I had neither the emotional nor the financial resources really to enjoy. It was a combination of these factors, coupled with the feeling that I was stuck, that made me pack my bags one day and leave England. I wanted to go to America, but that was not easy in those days, especially for an Indian actor who was unknown. I had no choice but to return to India. I did make one solemn promise to myself that, no matter what happened, I would not knowingly take what I thought to be retrogressive steps—for example, returning to the amateur stage in Delhi.

Neither the theater nor television had progressed, it seemed to me, from the days I was at university in Bombay, and the commercial Hindi cinema was a possibility in 1977, but I was reluctant to start up the ladder once again, and my Hindi was rusty. I felt that the Bombay film people were not kindly disposed to actors who had worked and trained abroad. They appeared disdainful of the West, while aping it at the same time. I couldn't figure them out, and I couldn't see myself as a hero in Hindi films required to dance and pursue heroines around a lot of trees and flowering shrubs. So I accepted a job as an assistant editor of a journal at the India International Centre in Delhi.

I was at the Centre for five years, until 1982, when I left to play Victor Mehta in David Hare's new play *A Map of the World* at the Adelaide Festival in Australia. I had no illusions whatsoever about the increased possibilities or more or ever better roles in India. By 1977, it was clear to me that work in India in the English language was neither possible nor acceptable in the wider context. However, while I was at the Centre, not acting at all, not even considering the possibility of ever doing so again, an important process was nonetheless taking place; I was shedding all the masks, all the baggage, all the things I was not. I became a person when the actor was gone.

CZ: Did you feel that the roles offered to you were greatly limited by your nationality? Or was there a general dissatisfaction with living in England, and a longing for home?

RS: By the middle of 1976, I felt I really did not have what it takes to be a "good" actor. I justified this pessimistic view of myself by thinking, perversely, that if I did have what it takes, then surely someone, somewhere would recognize that talent. But as I was getting little work and indifferent work, when I did get it, and as I was very poor, my logic seemed irrefutable. Add to all this a love affair that had become very hurtful, and you have a pretty lethal cocktail of circumstances. It was a stressful and depressing three-year period in the mid-seventies. Roles offered to me *were* limited by my nationality, though that was a professional limitation I had learned to live with. It never overly worried me. I realized that an Indian in search of roles in a mainstream culture was bound to be something of an anomaly and bound to be false, as the role would always be seen through British rather than Indian eyes.

CZ: You seem to have enjoyed a special relationship with David Hare, both in your starring role in A Map of the World, *and in your playing of The Fool in the Hare-directed production of* King Lear *for the National. Can you talk about your relationship to his work, and the sympathies you might share?*

RS: David Hare was in India for a while looking for suitable actors to cast as Victor Mehta at around the same time that the film *Gandhi* (1982) was released. He stayed with us, and I remember to this day my mother serving —in his honor—her version of bland English food. My wife, who is also English, refers to it as "grey food." Anyway, David and I talked—about India, about politics, about change, about myself. When he returned to London, he finished writing *A Map of the World* and offered me the leading role. The play opened in Adelaide, played a season at the Sydney Opera House, then opened at the Lyttleton Theatre as part of a National Theatre season. In 1985, it played the Newman Theater at the Public in New York. At each venue, the play was critically well received. The theaters were full, and I was enjoying myself for the first time in my professional life.

Victor Mehta was a character I could play from the center of my own experience. Indians amuse David. He finds their anarchy funny; their passion and excitable natures stimulate him. He finds the inherent tensions in Indian society interesting. He loves the politics of India—like great soap operas—and he finds a society trying to change, or rather living-in-change challenging to his own left-wing socialist views. I admire very much his impeccable theatrical taste and the sheer elegance of his writing, not to speak of his sharply incisive mind. David's inherent reserve prevented anything more than good matey-ness, but I am very, very fond of him.

The role of Victor Mehta is unarguably the most interesting, stimulating, and complex that I have played so far. At one level, Mehta is a bitter character, but his bite emanates from a very sensitive and kind heart. David particularly liked this side of Mehta and said to me one day, "If ever I do *King Lear*, I'd like you to play The Fool. It's Shakespeare's greatest play, I've always wanted to do it, but I won't do it unless I find a 'strong' actor to play the King."

Anthony Hopkins agreed to play King Lear when he was at the National, still playing La Roux in the hugely successful production of *Pravda*, with which Hare was associated. David knew *Lear* was a greenlight project. Of course, he had forgotten all about his offer of The Fool to me—it was five years since he had made it, perhaps even rashly. I happened to meet Hopkins at a BAFTA awards dinner in London, and I told him, conversationally, of David's offer. He repeated the story to David, who promptly offered me the role. I said, "It's going to be another six months or more before rehearsals begin; I'm off to India. Can you give me something to think about?" He said, "I want a bitter Fool." That's all David said. I had too long to think about that part with no support. That was a grave mistake. When rehearsals began, David said to me, "I've cut all the funny bits. No rhymes. No songs. No funny hats or props. No funny walks, no nothing. Just a bitter Fool in a black costume." It was a longer-than-usual rehearsal period—eight weeks. I think it would be true to say that rehearsals were dominated throughout by Hopkins' struggle with Lear. He wanted to shed the character of La Roux, but the harder he tried, the more Lear sounded and behaved like La Roux. David was kind and patient, but also frustrated. He wanted the production to follow some sort of pattern determined by his ideas. He ended up instead playing Mary Poppins to Anthony Hopkins' problems. Others in the cast were wiser and more experienced than I. They quickly found their characters and gave shape to their performances. I waited for Hopkins to acknowledge the presence of The Fool in the scenes they had together. I felt there was nothing I could do with The Fool in isolation, as everything The Fool does or says is in relation to Lear. Hopkins gave me the distinct impression that he considered The Fool to be some sort of pestilential housefly, that he would have liked to swat to death. There was time, and I thought something would happen miraculously. I was wrong. When the play opened, Irving Wardle, *The Times* critic, wrote that he didn't know what Seth was trying to do with The Fool. What he didn't know, of course, was that neither did Seth. I did not have a character, nor a performance. I did not know what The Fool was supposed to be doing or saying. I felt like that pesky housefly, except that no one was actually swatting me to death. I wish they had. I failed myself; I failed David

Hare. I failed utterly as The Fool. *Lear* played 100 performances and I don't know how I survived them.

I've brought the subject up on one or two occasions with Hare, but he squirms when I do, so I've stopped talking about it. What I've never said to David is that he failed me, too. He never saw how his conception of a bitter Fool was going to mesh with Hopkins' bull-in-a-china-shop King.

CZ: Moving on to your film work, perhaps we could begin with the father in My Beautiful Laundrette *(1985).*

RS: Characters like Papa in *My Beautiful Laundrette* are very common on the subcontinent. They are basically impractical. They have good minds. They have left-wing socialist views, and they are idealistic. In Papa's case, there was alcoholism, a failed marriage to an English woman, bitterness about his condition in England, and a great longing for "home," which was Pakistan. Hanif Kureishi had based the character on one of his uncles who lived in Karachi, and whom I met before filming began. The great difficulty with characters like Papa is that playing them with a British cast in a British context and with a British director makes them ring less true than if they were played in their own natural habitat of India or Pakistan. The success of that film, and indeed the character, was a complete surprise to all involved in its making. Stephen Frears, the director, said to me once that *Laundrette* grew in popularity after its release, like a mushroom growing in the dark. It took on a life of its own.

I particularly need the help of a kind and patient director to help me towards a fuller realization of the character in performance. Regrettably, the pace at which the majority of small budget work is carried out leaves no room for patient enquiry. That I find immensely frustrating.

CZ: Was there any difference between these experiences and working for a large-budget mega-film like Gandhi?

RS: For Nehru in *Gandhi* I had ten days for preparation, most of it being done as filming actually progressed. Because Richard Attenborough found himself with so many inexperienced film actors playing major roles, especially among the Indians, he was kind and helpful. Being an actor himself, he knew that help was required and, more importantly, he knew *how* to help. I am very proud of a scene towards the end of the film when a very harassed Nehru challenges an irate and angry mob who are calling for Gandhi's death. In that scene, I have somehow been able to get the spirit of the character. I say "somehow" because my portrayal of Nehru I feel was patchy. That part was played by me in the most extraordinary of personal circumstances, and it took almost everything I possessed just to prevent my knees from shaking. I learned something very important on that film, and that was stillness.

CZ: Do you have any particular way of approaching a script? How do you first read it and learn it? Do you do it mnemonically or by emotional association? Many actors say that they don't learn a script by heart before beginning a project, but prefer to learn it as they go along.

RS: I have no set way of approaching a script. It depends entirely on the time available. I read it as often as I can until my mind can flow easily from one scene to the next. Flow and rhythm, I think, are very important, because there you have your clues to the kind of story being told. Each reading aids familiarity with the material. I can relax only when I'm very familiar; I try to absorb the story and the characters in broad strokes. I try to allow the material to possess me—to enter my own thoughts and feelings. I don't learn a script or my lines. I *look* at them so that I can become familiar with them, so familiar that I don't need to think about them, like finding your way home. You just do it.

CZ: How do you begin to develop a character? If you are playing in a period piece, like Little Dorrit *(1988) or performing a nonfictional character, such as Nehru, how much research would you do? In films like* Mississippi Masala *(1992), did you speak or correspond with Indians who have lived in Uganda? Did you research Indians living in the Southern U.S.? Or do you feel it is up to the text to provide that information for you?*

RS: For the development of character, again, I have no set way. I am learning not to panic, learning that panic only makes you clutch at straws that can never, in the end, prevent you from drowning. I am learning to trust that things *will* happen. Little clues will pop up, memories will float by, bits of the jigsaw will eventually find a place in the larger picture. The character's specific voice has to come from the same center that produces your voice. I look for a physicality from my own limbs. I test rhythms that feel right for the character. I try to find the sorts of breath that will carry the right feeling for the character. Usually, there will be one key that will open all the other doors to the character. Finding that key is what is difficult. The rest will usually follow from it.

Many of the characters I play I'm unfamiliar with. Research and search are, therefore, very important for me but, as I've said, preproduction time is always predicated by the budget, and projects with relatively small budgets will never allow for luxuries like research. *Mississippi Masala*, for example, was shot first in America and then in Uganda. I did hear the very area-specific Ugandian-Asian accent when the film unit moved to Kampala, but by that stage two-thirds of the film had already been shot. What can one do? You make the best use of whatever you can: I stopped over in London for a day, on my way to the States, to talk to some Ugandan Asians in London. That was it.

CZ: How important is the political content of a piece to you? Would you play a character who had sympathies completely opposing your own, or espoused an ideology you were opposed to?

RS: Political content is of no importance for me. Playing characters opposed to my own sympathies and ideologies is not only very challenging but also very rewarding in terms of self-knowledge and broadening horizons. Beyond the limitations of one's conditioning lie all the shades of human possibility. Any opportunity to reveal hidden aspects of the *self* has to be enriching. I agree with Peter Hall that acting is the art of self-revelation. It is the bane of most actors' lives that they will never be stretched. One advantage to stardom is that you can call the shots and so provide the opportunities for stretching yourself.

CZ: How do you make a role personal for yourself? Do you use imagery, personal memories?

RS: I try to be watchful, to be ruthlessly honest in discarding anything that is false, that is not coming from my *true voice*. The term *true voice* lies at the center of the Iris Warren techniques of breathing and voice production that we were taught at LAMDA. One cannot breathe naturally until the body is in relaxation. The voice will not be "true" and free until the breathing is natural. Breath carries feeling. Breath gives you life. Without it, you are a corpse. I never understood all this fully in practice while I was at LAMDA. Bits of technique have been falling into place gradually over the thirty years since I was introduced to it. It has taken me years to learn that anything produced in one's head is useless unless it can be blended organically and un-self-consciously into one's entire being. So making a role personal has as much to do with technique as knowing my own mental and physical problems in order that these do not get in the way.

CZ: Do you feel there is a pattern, or has been a pattern, in the sort of roles offered to you? Have you found the roles offered to you as you mature more interesting?

RS: Yes. The pattern could be expressed as "educated, upper class, even aristocratic, socially self-confident Indian gentlemen or professionals." Directors and casting directors have said to me that they like the "compassion and humanity that emanates from behind my eyes." On the whole, the roles that have been offered to me and those that I have accepted since playing Nehru in *Gandhi* have been so varied and many-layered that I have never felt frustrated on that account.

CZ: What do you think makes great film acting?

RS: Simplicity. Mental and physical relaxation. Comfortableness in front of a camera. Focus. Truth of the moment. Character. Performance. Intelligence. Not necessarily in that order.

CZ: What do you feel you've learned about acting for the camera that has evolved over the years, that might be helpful to young actors?

RS: Never to inflect. Either vocally or while performing an action. This I've learned from watching American actors who have the advantage of speaking lines that don't require inflection. English, as spoken in Britain, relies on inflection to carry intent and shades of meaning. Indian culture inflects and colors most things. That shows in the kind of acting seen on the Indian screen. Simplicity, focus, uninflected speech, and action are best, I think, for the camera. It is astonishing how little you have to *do*. And yet simply *being* is so difficult. That is perhaps why animals and children are so beguiling in front of a camera.

CZ: How did you feel the first time you saw yourself on screen?

RS: I was irritated by my involuntary reactions to things like my nose, my teeth, my height, my stoop, my makeup, hair, clothes, and so on.

This is most unfortunate, but it emanates from cultures that do not tolerate blemishes. Look at *Baywatch* on TV. The camera loves beauty. The audience does, too. Yet the camera cannot distinguish true beauty from manufactured beauty or glamour. So even when an actor like Tom Cruise appears in a scene unwashed, unshaven, and smelly, he basically looks good. I often wonder whether a Spencer Tracey or a James Cagney had a greater struggle than a Clark Gable or a Humphrey Bogart. Film does glamorize what goes onto it. Perhaps a world without blemish is what our dreams are made of.

CZ: If you are playing a supporting role in a play or film, do you fill in a backstory for the character to make it more real for yourself? Can you give an example when you've done this?

RS: Supporting roles and, to a lesser extent, cameo roles, are very difficult. It's best to go for one striking impression rather than several subtle ones. My role as Amrit Rao, the barrister, in the closing minutes of Lean's *A Passage to India* (1984), worked because I gave the unequivocal impression that the character was very intelligent, confident, and bored.

CZ: You have acted in Indian films, and directed and acted in the Indian theater. Can you talk about the differences between acting in India and in England? I'm sure this is quite a vast topic.

RS: It is a major topic and at the heart of my own development. Aspects of Indian culture display great subtlety: religious and spiritual thought, for instance. Classical music is subtle; so, too, are some forms of poetry. Some visual art forms, on the other hand—sculpture, films, architecture—prefer overstatement, embellishment, and other such forms of excess and exuberance. I have had to learn by several trials by fire and by much personal humiliation and pain that the Indian approach to acting simply will not carry in the West. Spelling things out, coloring them, underlining them are rejected in Western filmmaking. In India, the fear is that subtlety on the screen may be missed altogether by the audience. You must be seen to act in order to act. You must appear made-up in order to look made-up. An Indian audience is also accustomed to "slowness," especially in the opening stages of a performance. A spiritual discourse, for example, by a guru in India is, by Western standards, a slow affair. Matters of great import or subtlety are slowly spelt out, and often repeated. Shakespeare, for instance, could not be understood at the pace at which it is spoken in England. In fact, an Indian audience will feel cheated if it cannot savor some of Shakespeare's great speeches. I'd go so far as to say that an Indian audience would get very restless if it felt it was being given a snack rather than a hearty feast. Most things are slower in India. In the West, I am always conscious of speed, of the audience, the directors, getting bored by slowness. Didacticism is a very dirty word in the West. Not so here. For me the dismantling of this cultural bias for slowness has been as painful as it has been long. Only once in my entire career as an actor has this business of "slowness" been confronted. It was Peter Brook who said that the closing moments of *A Midsummer's Night Dream* worried him, until he realized it was, in fact, a wind-down—the pace of the production had to lose, gradually, its outward energy until it came to a point of restfulness. In other words, he felt the production should leave the audience feeling at peace with itself in much the same way that a forty-minute meditation will leave one feeling.

CZ: You've worked within the Hollywood system several times. I was surprised to see you recently in a film with Jean-Claude Van Damme, someone I would not associate with you. Was it a challenge to work with a megastar?

RS: Yes. Because Van Damme has learned all the power games of Hollywood and its veneration of money. His films get seen and make a lot of money for the producers. He knows that. So he thinks he can be obnoxious and get away with it. They need him more than he needs them. But all tyrants fall, and so will he one day.

CZ: Have you ever had a battle of personalities between yourself and another actor or a director? How do you tend to resolve those "creative differences"?

RS: I will never forget the two occasions when I clashed with other people—one a director, the other an actor. In the first instance, I walked off the set. In the second instance, the actor walked off the set. Clashes can occur when caged feelings are not released. Release is often possible by a talk or a discussion. When bottled up, there is every likelihood of an explosion one fine day. Acting is an emotional business, usually done under stress or pressure. In my experience, the British prefer good behavior—outwardly, at least. Everyone likes to get on with each other, even if there's a lot of moaning behind the scenes. Good behavior can inhibit good work, which tends to come from an emotionally charged atmosphere, where danger and risk and extremes are all possible in an atmosphere of mutual trust. Americans are more tolerant of actors' tantrums, especially if they result in what is generally considered good work. In my view, the best work flows from a totally relaxed, friendly, and playful and unhurried working atmosphere. The Americans are better at that than the British, who are great sticklers for form and good behavior.

CZ: Has there been a time or times in any medium when you've felt your "creative juices" simply weren't flowing? What do you do in that case? Do you ever use improvisation as a means of unblocking a difficult area of a text or to develop your instincts?

RS: Very often the blockages can be removed by calming the mind, relaxing, not expecting anything to happen, talking, and, of course, improvisation. A point about improvisation—it is at best a group activity, and it will only yield benefits if the director as well as all the actors in a given scene want the improvisation, and are willing to surrender time for it. The British don't care much for improvisation, nor indeed for too much raw emotion.

The word *instinct* I find suspect. All adult humans are conditioned beings; their instincts long since blunted by social and cultural behavior. My use of the word *instinct* would apply to an actor who quickly recognizes that the work he is embarked upon is good and right, and falls within the bound of "good art." *Good art* is a relative term, but it seldom lacks control or grace, rhythm or integrity.

CZ: What do you think it is about the British character—if you think there is such a thing—that doesn't make heroes out of their actors, where acting is just a job, actors are regular blokes versus the American mentality, where stardom is the thing?

RS: Chiefly emotional reserve. More so with British men than women. It is bad manners and "not done" to boast and flaunt yourself in public. There's a right way of doing everything in Britain, and everything is done in that way, unless, of course, you're a deviant, in which case no one wants to know you.

Their acting is different because of their connection to language, especially to literature and poetry. It comes from the way in which the British express their thoughts, feelings, and ideas. It comes, too, from their particular intrapersonal and social interactions. British women will express their feelings more readily than men, especially in private circumstances. In society, they become more reserved. Understated feelings are a British hallmark.

CZ: What gives you inspiration right now, as an Indian actor working in English?

RS: In general, Indians writing stories in English with Indian characters began to be taken seriously only after the publication of Salman Rushdie's *Midnight's Children*. That was the first story I read in English by an Indian that I felt was about people like me. Since then, there have been several stories by several writers that I can identify with. So long as these writers are read in the English-speaking world, there is every indication that even more writers will appear, whether from India or from the migrant communities in the U.S., Canada, Britain, and Australia. This happy development has been the single most important thing to have happened for an actor like me. It now remains for us actors to keep pace with the writers and produce quality work that meets the very high standards in writing that have already been set.

Career Highlights

Film: *Gandhi* (BAFTAN) 82. *Indiana Jones and the Temple of Doom* 84. *A Passage to India* 84. *My Beautiful Laundrette* 85. *Partition* 87. *Little Dorrit* 88. *1871* 90. *Mountains of the Moon* 90. *London Kills Me* 91. *Mississippi Masala* 91. *Such a Long Journey* (GENIE) 98. *Vertical Limit* 2000. *Monsoon Wedding* 2001.

Theater: *A Midsummer Night's Dream* 72–73. *A Map of the World* 83–84. *King Lear* 86–87. *The Millionairess* 95.

Television: *Pravina's Wedding* 85. *Running Late* 92. *Stalin* 92. *The Buddha of Suburbia* 93. *Inspector Shaikh* 94. *Flight* 95. *Food for Ravens* 97. *The Turning World* 97. *Iqbal* 98.

Sir Peter Ustinov

It was really my mother who suggested that I should go into the theatre because I had a gift for imitation. I know the critics say there's a great difference between imitation and acting; I don't agree: What is acting but imitation of the imaginary?

CAROLE ZUCKER: What sort of cultural milieu were you raised in? And when did you first know that you wanted to be an actor?

PETER USTINOV: I don't know. It was really rather a negative approach. All my mother's family is deeply engaged in the arts. My mother herself was a painter and a scene designer, and so she had access to many theatrical people: dancers, musicians, and people like that. She even did sets for Covent Garden and for the Ballet Rambert; she did the designs for my first two plays. She was always in the wings somewhere.

It was really my mother who suggested that I should go into the theater because I had a gift for imitation. I know the critics say there's a great difference between imitation and acting; I don't agree: What is acting but imitation of the imaginary? You imagine something and you really imitate it, or at least you feel yourself in the bones of what you have imagined. To imagine a political figure or so on, and to do him justice, you have to make even a bigger stretch, because you don't resemble those people, necessarily.

CZ: What sort of schooling did you have?

PU: I was no good at school, I hated school; that's why I have a great deal of compassion for other people of my (then) age, who probably need to fend for themselves. I would say that there are some temperaments for whom bad education is the best thing, because they have to react against it.

I went to the kind of school which has mercifully altered completely now; I visit them occasionally, and they are now co-educational, and they're sensibly dressed, and, as a consequence, talking to the young people there is like talking to young adults. Whereas we were—I was very conscious of the fact at the time—overblown schoolchildren. I had to wear a top hat and tail coat, striped trousers, and carry a furled umbrella in my hand. It was probably my first education in paradox, because I never unfurled the umbrella, because I knew I could never fold it again afterwards, so I got thoroughly wet. My top hat had to be brushed in the right direction, and all that.

CZ: Can you describe the sort of child you were?

PU: I was always very nervous attempting things which I knew I couldn't do well, such as piano playing competitions, that I was hopeless at. Acting, I was a bit better, but I never had any possibility of doing it at school. In my prep school, I played a pig in a farmyard drama. The master at the end of term wrote to my mother and said that I had been "adequate" in the part of a pig. That was not really very encouraging. The other time, I was a nymph with golden tresses, set to lure Ulysses onto the rocks. I wasn't a bit surprised when he just sailed by.

CZ: I take it this was an all-boys school.

PU: Yes. Everything was all boys. Which explains quite a lot of the trouble with England.

CZ: Would you call your upbringing bohemian?

PU: Very. And very unsettled. At school, I was embarrassed to know that my parents really couldn't afford to send me to that school. I knew that certain sacrifices were being made, and often bills were not paid; I found it doubly useless, therefore. I think, at a certain time of life—and it varies with most people—what used to be called a "finishing school" is really terribly useful, because you can't really do anything positive yet, but you're aiming yourself on the launching pad. It's a difficult period. The idea of a period of gestation, of digestion of the ideas that you have received earlier on, is probably necessary before you launch yourself finally into life as it is.

I must say, when I was elected Chancellor of the University of Dundee, in my inaugural address, I said how sad I was that my father wasn't able to see me, having got into a university at last. I said my only way in was through the top, because all other ways were barred. I believe that children develop at different paces, and I'm now passionately interested in all sorts of things I couldn't give a damn about at school.

CZ: Have you found in your experience of working with actors as an actor, writer, and director that it takes a certain kind of personality to be an actor? Do you find a common thread among all the people who you know who are actors?

PU: No, I don't think it takes a certain kind of person because I think you can develop that. Some actors are from very surprising backgrounds. There are always misconceptions about acting. Aldous Huxley actually wrote that actors are, by definition—because of, I suppose, their calling—exhibitionists. I think the very opposite is true; public figures—statesmen, politicians—are the exhibitionists, because they like appearing as themselves, and making after-dinner speeches without notes. They love this kind of public preening; it does their egos good. But actors . . . I've always asked myself why Laurence Olivier, who was a seemingly very extroverted character, often wore a false nose, which bore a striking resemblance to the nose he had anyway, but was just pushed forward a bit. Why did he do it? I'm sure he did it as a feeling of hiding, a feeling of having a mask, of being unrecognizable, as being someone else. As witness, his maiden speech in the House of Lords was absolutely dreadful, because he tried to emulate Shakespearen speech. He felt he had to do something, because he had no nose on. I think actors are often very shy, even demure people.

CZ: You studied with Michel St. Denis. In your memory, what was the emphasis of the training?

PU: The training taught you that you had not only a voice and a mind, but also a body, and that you could act with the whole of your body. I think it was rather limited. It's curious to say that now, because I had a great affection for Michel St. Denis, but I don't think he really was a very good actor himself. That doesn't prevent one from being a good teacher, of course—on the contrary sometimes. But I found myself very frustrated, because it seemed to me an ungenerous way of teaching.

CZ: Why was it ungenerous?

PU: I had a very odd relationship with him, where he was usually rather damning of anything I tried to do, and the other masters round the back said, "Don't worry about him. You continue doing what you're doing." He tried to discourage me from leaving after two years, saying, "'You will never play anything, except perhaps understudy Shakespearean clowns,'" which is the one thing in the world I dread—not understudying, but Shakespearean clowns. I left all the same, and I'm very glad I did, because you really learn more outside drama school. But drama school is very useful because it makes you conscious of various things, and subjects, and ideas, which you either accept or reject; you take what you want out of the situation. I have, instinctively, more trust in people that find their own way, making use of what they're told, even by quarreling with it— especially by quarreling with it—than those who accept automatically all they're told and try to please their masters. People who try to please their masters rarely go as far in life as those who don't bother to.

CZ: In your autobiography, Dear Me, *you write, "My instinctive quarrel with the so-called method, valid to this day, is that so much of what is said, done, and thought during rehearsal is untranslatable into dramatic terms. This leads to the all-too-frequent phenomenon of actors who have reached devious and impractical conclusions about their roles, doing incomprehensible things with an aura of self-satisfaction, even authority, which not unnaturally tends to alienate an audience." You also talk about "the method" as being intelligence at the expense of instinct. What is this quarrel that you seem to have with "the method." The second point I want you to address is the perception that American actors act from the guts, whereas British actors are more technical and act from the head. You seem to be saying exactly the opposite thing—that "the method" is an intellectual technique.*

PU: I *am* saying that. If you say they act from the gut, it then becomes a question of energy; I think Americans are attracted towards the dramatic or even hysterical; they are often very good at hysterical scenes. The British aren't as good at that because they're more self-contained. And also, the priority given to the quality of language is different, of course. The Americans, I feel, sometimes are conscious of the fact that they are creating a tradition which creates its own excitement, of course, and is a very laudable thing. The English have done it, too. When I was young, everybody had to speak a kind of Oxford English. Since then, all sorts of regional accents have made their point, and, in fact, people like Albert Finney or Michael Caine, for instance, still talk with the accent they were born with; they've made no effort to hide that. And that, of course, gives the same kind of impulse as one has in America, because they are renewing a tradition instead of making it for the first time. The quarrel I have with the "method" is that they talk too much.

CZ: Do you mean they overintellectualize about their parts?

PU: Yes. I remember attending one of the sessions at The Actors Studio, because I hate to be in disagreement with something that I haven't fully understood, and Geraldine Page, who was an adorable woman, was rehearsing an improvised version of Strindberg's *Miss Julie*, and the actors described—for Lee Strasberg, who sat there with a tape recorder—the various feelings they had while rehearsing *Miss Julie*, and then they abandoned it because they were hungry, they ate, they had showers, because it was very hot, and then they settled down to attack *Miss Julie* again. The whole thing became so oppressive that I left and had time just to say quite quietly, "You need a lawyer." The only thing wrong was that Raymond Burr wasn't there with his wheelchair.

Time and again, I've come across this. It all started, of course, with the Russians, with Chekhov. The beginning was quite logical, as I also said in my book. In those days, if somebody opened a drawer and found love letters to his wife, he would stagger back two paces and put his hand to his heart. Chekhov came to the conclusion that nobody in real life does that. You open the drawer, you see the love letters to your wife, and you shut the drawer, and you want to make sure that she will not be able to notice that you've opened it. That changes everything. You don't react at first, because you have to think what to do in those cases. So all the Victorian business was thrown out of the window, and Chekhov was a great innovator in that, and Stanislavski of course. Now what's happened with the Moscow Art Theatre is that the prompt book from the original productions of Chekhov were kept religiously, like a bible. So if it said that the original actor at this point scratched his nose, he took a drink of coffee, he yawned, and then he went on, now this is being followed by people who have no feeling for it. The arteries have hardened, and the man gets to that line and says, "Uncle Vanya . . . [mimes drink of coffee, yawns]. . . . I'm going to Moscow tomorrow. . . ." That takes an awful lot of time.

CZ: There must be performers that you admire, people like Brando.

PU: Yes, because they belong to a new tradition. I directed a movie with Paul Newman. He's wonderful and, in many ways, unique at doing American parts, but some others are outside his range, and he therefore acts them with reverence, but no real guts. The same is true with Brando. I don't doubt that Brando can probably play a Chinese by now; he's got the dimensions to do all sorts of things.

CZ: What is your method? How do you research a role? You talk about the importance of the element of surprise, which I think is important for all actors doing a role for the first time, and you say everything emerges from "the psychological verity of what it is you're doing." How do you get to that truth?

PU: Well, you know the rails you're on, you know the instructions of the director, but within that framework, you must retain at all times the capacity to take yourself by surprise within the limits imposed by the form. As a dramatist, I have no objection at all to people taking initiatives on occasion, as long as I have the right to say, "Don't do that next time." Risk doing the wrong thing; You can always not do it, but you won't fall in our estimation if you go back on your word and say, "I was wrong." I think that's necessary. I think at least during rehearsals one should have every liberty, even at the expense of outraging everybody. You can always say, "I'm terribly sorry; I was just trying something."

CZ: What I'm getting at is that I think you need to understand the text, and have some ideas about it before you begin to "try something" or be playful. You have to have an understanding of the character before you can do variations in the way a character might behave or say a line. In essence, I'm asking what kind of research you do? You played Lear twice, and an historical figure like Herod, who certainly represents someone very far from you and your values. How do you research these people? How important is that sort of thing for you?

PU: Lear is always tremendously important because I've always had ideas about Lear which I haven't had about any other Shakespeare play, quite frankly. I find it very different to play Othello, even if I was convincing in other respects, simply because I think he's such an ass. I really think he's an idiot.

Lear fascinates me because I think he's mad at the beginning, where he makes these absurd judgments. I think he's probably slightly loaded after dinner, and he organizes this contest, and he's quite mad. The irony of the play, which I think is a wonderful one, is that the girls, the terrible girls, Regan and Goneril, are absolutely justified to keep him out with first of all fifty and then twenty-five men, and finally, with only the fool. Because as housekeepers, these men make such a mess, they're carousing all over the place, drinking, relieving themselves on the walls, I mean, terrible! So they're completely justified, and it's Lear's madness, and *folie de grandeur* that he keeps saying, "I'm coming next weekend, with only fifty retainers, so kindly clear out the left wing because I want if for myself," "Father, you belong in an institution." And gradually, owing to Lear's experiences, especially on the heath, he regains a sense of balance of what's happened. By then it's too late, and he suddenly realizes, at his age, how tiring it is physically, to be sane, because you have to answer to everything. So he takes refuge in a much more evident madness, which is not quite real, because through it, he recognizes Cordelia, but very discreetly. And he is quite lucid at the end, absolutely lucid.

CZ: Do you find that you have a desire to explore the dark side of yourself? You haven't done it that much in your career, but in Lear, *one would think you would be forced to do that.*

PU: In *Lear* I certainly did. Of course, *Lear* is a very curious example, because we started rehearsing with those books, which are standard editions, in which half the page is taken up by footnotes by eminent professors.

CZ: Who directed the production you were in?

PU: Robin Phillips, at The Shakespeare Festival in Stratford, Ontario, Canada. We saw eye to eye from the beginning, absolutely, that it should be done in Victorian England, because it's also a play about uniforms. It's not a play about night shifts, it's a play about uniforms and badges of rank, and orders and protocols. Also, it lends itself to that period very well—the stiffness of everybody. It's really a very early Victorian Gothic play. Some critic said I lacked the majesty of Lear; I don't think that Lear should have any majesty whatever. He's a king, but that doesn't mean anything. Look at the Queen now. Has she got majesty? "My husband and I [imitates Queen Elizabeth's voice]. . . ." Is that majesty? I don't know. It wouldn't be heard over the storm. I think Shakespeare's greatness is that he survives all periods, because the fascists can use him to prove their point, and so can the antifascists. Orson Welles can do Julius Caesar as a fascist pig, but Mussolini could have engineered something quite different! When one saw Thatcher at work, and the British government, you realize that *Julius Caesar* is fundamentally a very British play, and has nothing to do with ancient Rome whatsoever. They're not Italians, they're not Latins at all, they're very scheming English people with velvet daggers which turn out to be steel.

CZ: I had asked you about examining your darker side . . .

PU: The darker side of my nature is something which I really have not dealt with a great deal because there are certainly dark sides . . . . I'm basically an extremely serious person, but my way of being serious is often to conjure up laughter where I can.

CZ: How do you get your creative juices going if you don't feel like it?

PU: I don't. I have a very Russian Oblomovist sense. I can really do *fa niente* for a moment, then it palls, and I have to do something.

CZ: Has there ever been a role where you've said to yourself, "I'm at sea with this character; I really need help," and was there any help forthcoming?

PU: I usually find a technical way of getting through it, because things like that are challenges, too. I can't remember anything specific, except that I had to play Peer Gynt; I was the first one to play Peer Gynt on television live. Four and a half hours. At the beginning, it was tough, because I really had a tendency towards corpulence, and I was strapped into this costume, so I could hardly breathe. And I said, "Look, Mother, there's Ragnar's fjord, and big reindeers are leaping over. . . ." and I'll never forget this actor who had to come on . . . the rest of us are streaming with perspiration, the end of the play is already in sight, this poor wretch has to come on like a substitute in a football match, in the last two minutes, and he did something—he was a very distinguished actor—which I've never seen before: He blew his lines before he'd uttered them. He came towards me with a God-like look, and then the God-like look became vague, and started searching—this is all live, remember—and to save the situation, I said, "Are you not the button-molder?" He said, "Thanks. Yes. I am the button-molder." [laughter] Anyway, those are among the happier memories.

CZ: What would be the difference, for you, in working on an art film like Lola Montes *(1955) and working on a commercial project like* Death on the Nile *(1978)? And what would be the differences between working on a Hollywood studio film versus working on smaller European films?*

PU: Once you get on the set, there's really no difference. I've been quoted as saying they're very much like nightclubs: Once you're in the dark, you don't know where you are, really. But of course *Lola Montes* was different, because that was Max Ophuls, who had already had his brushes with Hollywood, and found the pressures there not at all to his liking. It was much more European in mind and spirit. A script like that would never be approved by Hollywood in a month of Sundays. Never. And, I thought not really terribly good. He made it good visually. And I know at the premiere—which was a disaster in Paris, because the film broke three times, and he roared with laughter every time it happened—he foresaw disaster, but he did say that Martine Carole was pretty empty in the role, and he justified it to me by saying, "The emptier she is, the better." That was an intellectual consideration which didn't get as far as the footlights, really, if you know what I mean. At the same time, working with him had a fascination which I never had from any Hollywood director.

CZ: Can you describe that fascination in more detail? In a French interview you did, you said that you appreciated Ophuls without agreeing with him, and that the baroque excess made you nauseated.

PU: I said that it made me feel like part of a Swiss watch, and a very ambitious part, which wanted to know what the other parts were doing. Maybe I'm straying from the point, but I don't think so, because very often a detail of this sort will give you a much clearer impression of what the experience was really like: There was a point when we had eight hundred extras, I think. So we're not talking about the smaller dimension of European film. I knew they were running out of money, because they hadn't paid me. On one occasion, I had a very long take—over four minutes in one piece—in which I had to climb a spiral staircase and sing a song written by Georges Auric, and go on singing at the top. Well, as I started out on take one, I felt that I had a frog in my throat coming, and I was getting near the foot of the stairs, and I said to a German dwarf, "*Eine glasse wasser, bitte.*" He said "*Wasser,*" and he went off on these bow legs to get it. He got back to me with a glass of water as I was already above the first step, so we just managed to reach each other, and I took the glass and climbed the steps, singing the song with the glass of water, and got to the top, and stood there, still with the glass of water, and sang it to the end, and it all went in one take, and the extras applauded, because it seemed such a difficult thing to do. I went down, I must say, flushed with a little sense of triumph, went up to Ophuls, who was in his chair and evidently sulking—he wouldn't look at me—and said, "Well, how was it?" He turned away. I said, "What is this childish performance? You've got to tell me one thing or the other." He turned back and he looked at me rather sadly and said, "I wish I'd thought of that."

CZ: Have there been directors that you've felt were particularly helpful in their work with actors? What do you consider an ideal director–actor relationship?

PU: It obviously helps if there's a mutual admiration, without it becoming a clubby thing. It helped in all those De Niro films; he's obviously very close to Scorsese. This helps enormously. I was very fond of working with Fred Zinneman, for one very good reason: that he is the opposite of the director who knows precisely what he wants. He works more by a process of elimination; he knows what he doesn't want, and after that, he's feeling his way towards what he wants. That's the way an actor works also, and you do something for him which he either likes or dislikes, and he tells you so, and you maybe discuss it briefly. He doesn't talk very much; he'd "rather you tried it again." At the end you know that if it's passed his particular standard, it must be all right. He gives you a feeling of assurance from a basic feeling of mutual insecurity, which is shared. In other words, he makes the whole thing a mutual adventure, which is the thing you ideally would like to feel.

CZ: What, for you, is the biggest difference between acting for the film and theater?

PU: Well, you've got to remember that in theater acting, there are conventions which have to be accepted. You always talk much too loud for the first row, because otherwise the last row won't hear. They know that, and they accept that. The difference is that, in films and television, all the public are in the same seat, which makes an enormous difference. And, therefore, things that you can't do in the theater, such as raise an eyebrow, nobody's going to see that, but in a film, they see it at once. You can become much more sensitive in your acting for film, and even inaudible, because you very often know what is meant, regardless of whether you understand the words or not.

CZ: Do you feel that you have a tendency to be big or grand as an actor? There are some parts that you play on film where your performances seem very theatrical to me. I don't mean that in a pejorative sense.

PU: No. That seems to bother some Americans. I always get the same result from *The New York Times*. It's always the same critic, Mr. O'Connor, who says, "His usually hammy self suits him this time." I've really learnt much more in my career from the public than I have from even the wisest of critics, which is natural. I don't think anybody can quarrel with that. I know when a thing's going well; you know it, without having to be told.

CZ: Do you feel that the press in North America and in Europe treat you differently?

PU: Critics generally don't treat me terribly well. I think I irritate them because I'm very difficult to pigeonhole, and because I'm cheery and plump. There, we can go back to Charles Laughton. Laughton was often accused of overacting. But with a face like that, you were overacting if you were still! I always thought my Oscars for the Best Supporting Actor really meant the Best Fat Actor.

I have the capacity of being big, but I reign it in as often as possible. But when I played something very reasonable, like in *The Comedians* (1967), everybody was disappointed that I wasn't more in evidence! I was gratified because I got a very good notice from Alec Guinness in his autobiography, saying it was a wonderful performance. But I didn't do anything with it; all I had to do really was to slap Elizabeth Taylor's face. But even that took considerable effort.

CZ: Let's talk about your filmmaking. You've said on many occasions that you don't consider film an art form. Can you talk about that? Do you consider acting for film an art?

PU: Oh, film is an amalgam of all sorts of art forms, but it isn't really an art form in itself. I think largely because a play remains a play once it has been performed, and it can always be performed by other people. You get a different play, but you still get an art form. You get a fundamental design, like you do in building a boat or a house, as an architect. But with a film, if I get the money to do a film today, and I pick my cameraman, and he is not free, that already is a change of my initial concept and hope. Now, it's becoming more of an art form because the director can see the result immediately. Before, he couldn't. I remember working with [Henri-Georges] Clouzot, who had a reputation for great intelligence, which seemed to me to be highly doubtful. But dealing with him as a director, I found very peculiar. There, suddenly, the camera operator—all French, of course—said, "Cut it," and Clouzot, who was used to saying, "Cut it," because it was no good, said, "What the hell are you doing? Why are you cutting it? I liked it." And the cameraman said, "You can see the whole thing but I can see the frame, and you wouldn't have liked it on screen." That's really what I mean about it not being an art form: Clouzot was forced to do it again, although he liked what he had done, because, in the end, his conception might not have worked on the screen.

CZ: Is it your belief that any work that's collaborative is not an art form?

PU: No, I think it's a different kind of art form. It's not clearly a thing which can be the responsibility of one person. Now it's becoming more so because of the ability to see the result immediately on video monitors, and to decide it's not right or it's good enough.

CZ: When you have worked as a director, what was your strategy in working with actors? What are your feelings about rehearsing actors for film as opposed to theater?

PU: I think the great thing which is common to both is that there are many very good actors who give you exactly what they rehearsed, which is one thing. There are actors who are better than that who give you the impression that whether it's on the stage or whether it's in film, it is actually happening for the first time at that moment. That seems to me a vital thing. Rehearsal is fine, so long as you don't use it as a cushion, and just do what you rehearsed. If the thing has the element of surprise in it, which it always ought to, then you've got to allow yourself to be surprised for the first time by whatever it is, and disguise the fact that you've rehearsed it to death.

CZ: As a film director, do you ask for rehearsals?

PU: It depends on the circumstances. When I did *Billy Budd* (1962), I never had any rehearsals, because the stage was exactly the same all the time, there was no way of getting off the boat, you knew where you were, and they knew their characters very well.

CZ: In doing Billy Budd, *you were dealing with a complete newcomer, Terence Stamp, and you also were dealing with very experienced actors. How would you cope with that difference? How would you talk to Terence Stamp as opposed to Paul Rogers or Robert Ryan?*

PU: Directing, anywhere, is a function which is slightly like being a psychiatrist because you're dealing with people of vastly different temperaments. Some people like tension; others hate it. Some people feel masochistic enough to get the best out of themselves if they're abused and bullied and all the rest of it, which I hate doing. I'm no good at that. I always try and instill in them a sense of mutual adventure as important: "We're all in this together; feel free to say anything to me and I'll feel free. . . ." In the case of Terence Stamp, he was absolutely sure he hadn't got the part, because he was so tongue-tied when came to see me. The more he did that, the more I was convinced this was the only man who could do it, because he was doing exactly what the boy did. I warned everybody else that he'd never done a film before. I thought he was great in his audition.

This is one of the amazing things: Terence Stamp played the embodiment of total good, which is not a dramatic thing, because really it doesn't exist, and Robert Ryan played the part of total evil, which doesn't exist either. That's why I put in a scene there where they were attracted to each other's point of view, in order to humanize them, in order to have some sort of material to work with. Robert Ryan, in life, was an extraordinarily pure character, and Terence Stamp, when you meet him, is the last person you would choose as being an embodiment of total good. So it's a miracle of the screen that these extremes were conquered by people that were really, physically unsuited to them. And even mentally, which is more important. I was in the film because I was the only actor I could get at the price.

CZ: Do you ever see your earliest performances in film now? I was watching Private Angelo *(1949) and* Odette *(1950) at the British Film Institute. How do you feel that you've changed over the years, as an actor?*

PU: I had to work on my voice a lot. My voice now is extremely flexible; that's why I can sing Bach cantatas and things like that. That's one thing I notice, that my voice was pitched much higher in those days than it is today. I think I've probably become more selective in the possibilities, at this point. I think every phase has its own characteristics, so I've no sense of an arc, exactly. And there's no guarantee one hasn't lost something as well as winning something, that would be only fair. But now, of course, curiously enough . . . as Beethoven says, "If one is limited in some respects, it makes the other aspects of oneself sharper, more acute." I find it very difficult to walk long distances; I can stand for two hours on the stage, but in a cocktail party I have to sit down after three minutes. But that's normal, because there's no focus, and the mind is really very important in all these things. I think probably I can be more objective; probably when I was younger, I was more defiant, more eager to prove something. Now I'm not eager to prove anything at all.

It's also very interesting, when you get to my age, you begin to wonder about the immortality of the human soul, not because you're frightened of death or anything, but because you're very conscious of a palpable drifting away of the body and the spirit inside it. I call it the soul. Because the soul doesn't age at all; I'm sure I have the same soul as I had when I was two or one or none. All that's happened is that it's stuck for the moment in a body which I consider very much like a Hertz rent-a-body, which, when you received it, you went to the girl at the counter and said, "Have you anything with a slightly sportier engine? Or a sliding roof perhaps?" And they said no, they're all out, "Take that or leave it." "I'll take it! I'll take it. . . ." And you're stuck with something which you're used to, because you're used to moving your hands, everything is connected, but as you get old, it becomes not necessarily always a friend. Because you hear creaks in the coachwork, you drive it with rather more prudence, and your only hope is to bring it back to the counter again with dignity before you leave, and not have to leave it out in the countryside with a red triangle behind it. In point of fact, I think that explains a great deal of the activities of dirty old men, for instance. They don't realize that they're different. They're relying entirely on the soul! They never look in the mirror, because they wisely want to preserve that prerogative.

CZ: There seems to me to be a tendency among British actors to want to be perceived as ordinary blokes, that they can go down to the pub with the locals and bend an elbow, even if they're Sirs and Lords. Albert Finney has said, "Acting is mucking about in makeup." I was wondering where that comes from, that wish to be perceived as ordinary, even when one is very gifted.

PU: I think it's inherent. Even Beethoven said, "The gutter—it's from that vantage point that I can see life as it really was." In those days, of course, musicians were regarded as servants, even cultivated musicians. They were on the payroll of castles and things, as servants. Actors, it's always been the same thing. I know in my own family tree, there are two blank entries. One is "Married a Bolshevik," and the other one is "Married an actress." It was always considered that the line between acting and prostitution was practically nonexistent, and I think this extends to males as well. It's in the Victorian days where, first of all, it was decided that Sir Henry Irving would be a Sir. But still, this aura of ordinariness . . . Charles Laughton would say to me, "Acting is whoring." That was his impression. He very kindly referred to me as the Crown Prince, which meant, of course, "I am the King, although I'm a whore." So I think their position in society is never very clear, although it has bettered itself. I think actors are better off when they're pretending to be just ordinary folks. Because, after all, they get their inspiration from ordinary folks as often as not. Albert Finney is an ace example. His father was a bookmaker, I think, and he lives with that kind of ambience most relaxedly. Not everyone can be John Gielgud [does a superb Gielgud impression].

Career Highlights

Film: *One of Our Aircraft Is Missing* 42. *The Way Ahead* 44. *Quo Vadis?* (GG, AAN) 51. *We're No Angels* 55. *Lola Montes* 55. *Spartacus* (AA) 60. *The Sundowners* 60. *Billy Budd* 62. *Topkapi* (AA) 64. *The Comedians* 67. *Hot Millions* 68. *Logan's Run* 76. *Death on the Nile* 78. *Evil Under the Sun* 82. *Lorenzo's Oil* 92. *Salem Witch Trials* 2001.

Theater: *Crime and Punishment* 46. *The Love of Four Colonels* 51–52. *Romanoff and Juliet* (TonyN) 57. *Photo Finish* 62–63. *The Unknown Soldier and His Wife* 73. *Who's Who in Hell* 74. *King Lear* 79–80. *Beethoven's Tenth* 83–84. *An Evening with Peter Ustinov* 90–present.

Television: *The Life of Samuel Johnson* (Emmy) 57. *Barefoot in Athens* (Emmy) 66. *A Storm in Summer* (Emmy) 70. *13 at Dinner* 85. *The Well-Tempered Bach* (EmmyN) 85. *The Old Curiosity Shop* 94. "Victoria and Albert" 2001.